Expelled from Uganda

Noreen Nasim

Copyright © 2021 by Noreen Nasim

All rights reserved. No part of this publication may be reproduced, distributed or transmitted in any form or by any means, without prior written permission.

Dedicated to my daughter, Arya.

CHAPTER ONE

4th August 1972 - Kakira, Uganda
Age 19

Thunder bellowed, the voice of the chasing storms penetrating the ground, forcing me to stumble in the wet, red clay. My heart was questioning its true boundaries; a djembe drum, pounding against my ribcage. My shoes stuck to the ground, slowing my pace. Lightning struck, with adjacent trees crashing amidst embers. It was growing dark, and I needed to get home fast to tell them all. With my hair soaked and my forehead dripping with sweat, I thought about the horrifying information the boys had bombarded me with.

Were the boys telling me the truth? Or was it a rumour, out of control?

I could see my house on the horizon. It seemed like an eternity away. Rain hammered against the corrugated iron roof like nails pouring down from the heavens, piercing holes in our lives; puncturing our happiness. My Alsatian, Rocky, barked in his backyard kennel, troubled by the monsoon's wild display. Bursting in through the front door, stumbling down the hallway, I leaned, panting, against the decayed living room door frame.

"Idi Amin—ninety days—just—heard," I gasped, choking on my last word.

Maa stood quietly holding a glass of water, her lips

taut, her face displaying the Indian death stare. If looks could kill, Indians would have no surviving offspring. One solid dose was enough to have you quivering. For me, the stare was as routine as wild waves punishing its rocky shores. For one thing, my mother didn't approve of long hair on an adolescent man.

"What men keep their hair shoulder length? One day, I'll chop it off while you're sleeping, I'll tell you now," she would say.

However, I aspired to the Beatles' fashion statement. They were supreme and so was their hair. That night it was the sticky mud I'd trailed into the house, or perhaps that I'd bunked work at the garage to watch a movie with friends, that had triggered those deadly waves once again. Maybe Rocky had wrecked the backyard. That gigantic dog was a hyperactive mess-maker, but so lovable.

The crackling of the TV tuning in was drowning out the rants of my younger brother Kabir arguing with our little sister Shafina on the settee over who got to eat the last piece of mandazi. We rarely had mandazi in the house. A fluffy cake like dessert. Its texture was so soft, like that of a silk pillow.

"Shh… be quiet! Everyone settle down. We need to listen," my father instructed, staring at the TV down his long sharp nose through lenses so small they'd be fit for a caterpillar.

My siblings immediately hushed, fixing their gaze on the TV. Maa instantly released me from the talons of her glare and turned towards the hazy black-and-white image. Something told me that was a temporary reprieve. There he was. Idi Amin, the man himself. His eyes snakelike. His voice thundered with no microphone necessary.

- "I have decided to expel all the Asians from this country. Uganda must be for Ugandans only, and the economy must be run by Ugandans. The British are responsible for this. They brought the Asians here to build a railway. That railway is now complete. Britain will have to take responsibility. Uganda has been exploited. I give the Asian people 90 days to leave. Just wait and see what happens to them if they don't leave. Just watch!"

The metallic hammering of the rain engulfed the room, washing over my paralysed family. A rusty metal pail in the corner finally began to overflow, trickling rusty water onto Maa's prized rug; a wedding gift from her father, a family heirloom. That mystical rug, she often told me, brought luck to those who cherished it.

"This rug was the reason we were blessed enough to move to a bigger home. The blessings of our ancestors will always be with us as long as we protect it," she would proudly state.

At that moment, it didn't seem to be working.

"He can't do this," my father blurted, shattering the silence. My father was a man of few words and seldom displayed any sentiments of anger. We were all surprised to witness such a surge. His towering, lean build made it easy for him to project when he needed to.

"He can do whatever he chooses, he's the President," Maa replied with a bland expression and a sceptical flicker in her eyes.

"By force, Julekha! He *seized* power. He's not a President, he's a bully," my father yelled, folding his arms in a tight lock.

"But a bully in power, my dear, there's nothing that

will stand in his way. We are at his mercy," Maa replied, seeming uncertain.

Although to me and my siblings, my mother was 'Maa' and my father was 'Adha', my mother's name was Julekha, Jilu for short, and my father's name was Ismail. Maa would never address him by his name. In conversation she would refer to him only as *'my child's father'*. Anything else was a sign of disrespect, a damaging thing for an Indian woman's reputation in those parts. Maa tried her best to stick to Indian traditions and cultural practices. Much to our displeasure, this was all seasoned with superstitious behaviour. Maa would often sneak up on me, and poke her brass eyeliner applicator behind my ear, almost piercing my cartilage with its point.

"Stop resisting and let me apply this! It will ward off 'nazar', (evil eyes) and all other malicious omens. Gallivanting all day in the village. Goodness knows whose evil glares are upon my children."

"Jilu, what are we going to do?" Father enquired intently.

He looked confused. I'd never seen my father as worried as he was in that moment. It was disconcerting.

Before Maa could respond, I burst out, "Are we going to live in England?"

Kimo, my best friend, had moved to a place called Leicester in England. I must have sounded too excited by the notion because Maa snapped.

"Nobody is going anywhere! First, we find out whether this is true, then we will consider what we need to do. For now, you two need to stop arguing over food." Maa finally returned to her senses, her eyes first latching on to my siblings and then the muddy mess I had made. "It's not like we don't have enough to eat. Kabir, Shafina, stop behaving like animals. And you! Amir Ali Majothi. If you don't get that muddy mess cleaned up, I will bury you in the backyard myself."

"Where's Johari? Why can't she clean it up?" I sputtered, gazing down at the muddy tiles. Maa's death stare was too powerful to attempt to match it with my own.

"Johari needs a break from this mad house too, poor woman. She's having a few days off. Amir, you're nineteen years old, you're not a child. Start behaving like a sensible young man, and will you please cut your hair!" Maa fumed.

We promptly vacated the living room. When Maa screamed an order, we knew she meant business. I dragged my feet to the kitchen in search of something to clean up the mess, not realising I'd left a fresh trail of mud behind me.

Maa was a domestic trojan. She'd developed a military persona. I guess she had no choice with four feral children. The thought of cutting my hair made me cringe though; something I'd continue to fight.

My brave sentiments melted upon thoughts of Idi Amin's public speech. The pit of my stomach felt warm as my anxieties consumed me. Though no one spoke after the speech, Amin's words circled our minds like vultures conspiring to ambush me and my family.

Would he really expel all Asians from Uganda? I thought. *Does he have the power to remove more than 80,000 people? Do they even have Mango trees in England? What about Bollywood movies? I guess I could live off James Bond and John Wayne. But I can't do without Dev*

Anand and Rajesh Khanna. They're my heroes.

Eventually I became distracted from the scrubbing. So, I seized my opportunity, dropped the muddy rags, and crawled into my room. Retiring to my compact quarters every night was blissful, even though I shared it with my younger brother Kabir. I'd often pick up my acoustic guitar, reciting Bollywood melodies. Kabir didn't mind the tunes and we would occasionally have a singalong. Shafina would often twirl one of Maa's sequined scarves while strutting her favourite dance steps. My elder brother Aziz joined in the fun when he was around. He would often be occupied at Adha's garage till late hours; his head stuck under a bonnet and his overalls drenched in engine oil.

The storm continued that night; an unfamiliar sound. I always loved the grey tones before a torrential downpour. Electricity in the atmosphere prepared nature, conjuring excitement for what lay ahead. But that night, fear had replaced all contentment. What lay ahead for us was unimaginable.

CHAPTER TWO

1962 - Kakira, Uganda
Age 9

"Let me go, you jerk."

"I'm not a jerk. My name is Hero. You got that?"

It was difficult to see past the mountain of children huddled in the schoolyard. All I could distinguish within the clouds of dust were khaki backpacks clustered around a centre point. Eventually, I elbowed my way into the middle, only to find two silhouettes tumbling around in dry, red soil. One of them was Hero. Nobody knew his actual name. He'd flunked the same class four years in a row and was now repeating it for the fifth time. His father, a placid, frail vegetable merchant, had been called into school frequently to discuss Hero's behavioural issues. If it wasn't the vandalised classroom furniture, it would be graffiti on the corridor walls. The week before, it was due to stealing lunch tiffins from the year below. Where possible, I kept my distance from this infamous bully.

Hero sat on top of his most recent victim, clutching him by the throat. I turned to the boy next to me.

"What's his problem? Why does he have to pick on everyone?" I ranted, gritting my teeth.

"He's just setting the pecking order. New year, fresh students. I suppose he wants to show everyone who's boss," the boy shrugged.

Someone needed to put him in his place.

The faint flash of a Bollywood fight scene streamed before my eyes as I bolted off in the opposite direction. Rooting around the yard, I searched for a weapon. Large sugarcanes littered an adjoining picket fence, overlooking a field. They were perfect.

Barging through the crowd this time, I made my way to the centre again, in what felt like slow motion.

"Hero!" I yelled, shrieking like a banshee. In my head I sounded like Dev Anand, in reality I was just a nine-year-old boy—a screeching, feeble fledgling. Charging towards Hero, his victim still pinned to the ground, I delivered a sharp strike to his head.

"Aagh! You dog! I'll kill you," Hero roared, clasping his skull as he rolled around on the floor, like a turtle on its back.

"Oh yeah? Let me see you try!" I yelled, before delivering another blow to his bottom. He howled in pain, letting go of his head and gripping his bruised butt cheeks.

The crowd cheered. Even the faint sound of children booing had transformed into positive chanting.

A series of further scuffles and blows generated a dense, dusty fog.

Momentary anticipation swept the congregation. As the dust cleared, Hero became visible, having dropped to his knees. He babbled something under his breath through the muddy tears; perhaps an apology, but then shot off like a gazelle who'd spotted a crocodile at the water's edge. I wanted to grab him by his collar and make him apologise to the boy he'd pinned to the ground.

"Thank you. You saved me," a timid voice muttered.

"That's ok. His lesson was long overdue," I replied, dusting off my khaki shorts and white shirt, which wasn't so white anymore.

"He needs to go," came the voice again.

The dirt had settled and most of the children had dispersed. I turned to the junior student and introduced myself.

"I'm Amir," I said, finally seeing the boy's full appearance. He had jet black hair, oiled from left to right with a distinctive side parting. Despite the rough and tumble of the fight, his hair stayed in place the entire time. Of course it had! It looked like his mum had emptied half of Kakira Oil Mill onto his head.

"Kamlesh. But you can call me Kimo," he muttered, shaking my hand.

"Wait, I've seen you," I whispered, as though to myself; my eyes scanning him for clues. "I've seen you on my school bus. You're from Kakira Oil Mill county, aren't you?" I asked, trying not to laugh at the coincidence and trying even harder not to focus on his hair.

There were many little village areas within Kakira, the Oil Mill area was one of them. Every village area had its own bus, privately owned by the school, taking pupils to school and back every day.

"I've seen you in the bus queue," I said.

Kimo was always perched in the front seating area. The back seat was the King's throne. You had to be super cool to get a regular spot there.

"Yes, that's where I live. I've also seen you before," he said shyly. "You were with your brother and some friends last week, outside the tailor's. I saw you do a card trick and then collect money from everyone who watched," Kimo said, braving a grin.

Card tricks were a source of income for me. One shilling per spectator was the rule. Maa regularly sent me and Aziz on errands to the local tailor. Often to collect our own mended clothing; torn from playing outdoors, climbing trees, and inevitably fighting at school.

"So, you saw me, grafting. Do you want me to teach you some card tricks?" I chuckled.
"Yes, Miah, teach me!"
"Miah?" I asked.
"Miah means respected Muslim gentleman. You're Muslim, I can tell from your name. And you're definitely a gentleman," he smiled.
"Ha ha! I see. Ok, Kimo, from now on we're brothers. I'll teach you everything I know," I said.

The bell sounded one o'clock in the schoolyard, and it was time to return to our classes. We strolled together towards the school building. Sweltering heat from the midday sun set the ground glowing like magma. Tired and lethargic, I wondered if I could get away with napping under my desk, without Mr Desai catching me out, again. Kimo jabbered on about some girl who threw chalk at him the other day, as I zoned out and imagined myself as John Wayne, walking away from an epic battle in the middle of the American desert. My cowboy swagger was perfect with my skinny pin-like legs in my little khaki shorts, strutting through the dusty and humid school yard.

The weekend had arrived, and I was miserable for having been caged in my room. Frequently grounded on the best days of the week, I moaned about the unfair treatment. The reason behind my detention hung on the back of my bright orange bedroom door, covered in mud with a big tear across the pocket. Although my room was my haven, at times like that I wanted to escape. My stubborn nature cajoled me to do the opposite of everything I should do. A miniature vigilante within, constantly fighting for justice. Maa often referred to it as *middle child syndrome*, seeing me as the displaced, wild one.

"It's just a shirt. It can be washed and sewn back up," I grumbled, rolling my eyes.

Justifying quick fixes in my head for the damaged shirt didn't last long. A pebble shot across the room like a bullet.

"What the—"

Another one came charging in through my open window, having missed the jug on the dresser by inches.

"Who's doing that?" I shrilled, bouncing off my bed, racing towards the window. My instinct was to throw something back but, other than Maa's ceramic jug, there wasn't much to hurl.

"Miah! It's me, Kimo!"

My frustration turned into relief. I knew that voice. Better yet, Maa's jug had survived.

"What are you doing, Kimo? I was about to launch something right back at you," I whispered, realising we'd perhaps been a little too noisy.

"I'm here to get you out. I heard you got grounded for fighting with Hero."

"Shh.... don't say that out loud. My parents don't know I've been fighting. They've grounded me because my shirt was dirty and torn. I told them I fell," I said, wondering if they'd believed my fabricated tale.

"Oh... okay. So d'you wanna to sneak out?" Kimo proposed.

"I can't. What if I get caught?"

"But your dad won't be back from the garage until six o'clock. Let's go out, we can be back before then," Kimo pressed.

Maa was busy in the kitchen. Aromatic flavours had been floating into my room for hours. She would be there until late evening preparing samosas with two of her friends. A local wedding was taking place the very next day on our street. Most ladies in our village would be occupied preparing sweet snacks, clothing, and paper decorations.

"Ok, let's do this," I said, as I climbed onto the window sill. "Kimo, you need to crouch down. My feet won't reach the ground."

"Miah, I'm ready, go for it."

With my thin and nimble frame, I dropped my feet on to Kimo's back, like a stepping stool. Sneaking out of my temporary jail cell was instantly refreshing. Visions of being in my own western movie played in my head.

We galloped down the street, past the oil mill, as if fleeing from enemy bandits. We finally caught our breath underneath a giant mango tree. The sun was at its peak, like a clay oven cooking fluffy tandoori naan breads.

We were both salivating at the juicy appearance of

ripe mangoes dangling above us in the comfort of the leafy shade. Kimo licked his lips, not realising he'd dribbled a little. Maybe it was just sweat or perhaps excess oil from his head. Before I could ask him why his hair was always greased down, he displayed the same grin from earlier on.

"You want a mango don't you, Kimo?" I said, rolling my eyes.

"We can have whatever we want. Teamwork, Miah." Kimo winked and went in for a high five, confident that I was already on board.

He gave me a leg up and I climbed as far as I could. Having plucked some heavenly looking mangoes, I threw them down to Kimo, who had his shirt flared out like a sailor's net, ready for his catch of the day.

On my way down from the tree, I briefly pondered whether Maa had been in my room to check on me or not. *Could she have figured out that I'd gone? Would I get into trouble when I got home?* I could feel myself slipping; tightening my grip in desperation, but it was too late.

I lost all balance. BANG!

"Miah! Are you ok? Miah, Miah Answer me," Kimo yapped, frantically shaking me.

"I'm fine, relax. You're behaving like my mother," I said, moving his hands out of my way.

Whilst dusting down my clothes, I caught sight of what would likely be the root cause of my slaughter that night. My shirt pocket had been torn, and my collar shredded.

"I guess you've got the rest of the day to enjoy before—"

"Before Maa kills me, you mean? Yes!" I chimed in, unimpressed. I let out a huge sigh, before pursing my lips together for a moment.

"Let's at least eat these darn mangoes. They've come at a high price... we might as well enjoy them."

CHAPTER THREE

6th September 1972 - Kakira, Uganda
Age 19

"And that's how it's done, boys," I boasted, as I laid down a royal flush.

"Lunchtime is over. Get back to work!" a loud siren ploughed through my moment of victory.

"Adha, five more minutes," I pleaded.

"I said get back to work... and cut your bloody hair, Amir."

I ran my fingers through my locks with a cocky smile.

"I wouldn't even cut it if Paul McCartney himself told me to," I muttered

"What was that?" Adha snapped.

"Nothing Adha," I sputtered, averting my gaze.

"The rest of you boys need to stop losing all your money to this con artist. You'll never win at his silly card games, so why bother? Come on, we have to finish Kishore's car, pronto. He'll be back soon," Adha said, tossing a rusty wrench into his battered tool-box.

The garage housed a maximum of five cars at once. The odour of engine oil not only hung in the air, but stuck to our overalls, flavouring our regular doses of chai in greasy teacups. Tired wooden windows, with their decaying shutters were kept locked at night with rusty chains and bolts, to keep the place secure. Working for my father was the luxury deal of a lifetime, as I could kick back with a magazine whenever I wanted, and also head out with friends to catch a movie before closing time. Generating extra pocket money from fellow mechanics who worked there was a bonus. I often wondered whether I'd own the place one day. Thoughts of expanding the building would set me off daydreaming. A little cafe was my goal; attached to the side of the property, serving freshly fried samosas, sweet mandazi and onion bhajis. The thought of food was making me salivate again, even though we'd wiped our tiffins clean only ten minutes ago.

"Stop working!" A shout echoed through the garage.

The clattering of metal halted. We each made our way cautiously towards the doors.

"Kishore! What happened to you?" I yelled, shocked by his appearance.

"That's Uncle Kishore to you," Adha corrected me with a fractional death stare. He didn't have time to administer the full dose.

Culturally, anyone who was old enough to be your uncle or aunt, even if they were just an acquaintance of the family, would always be referred to as 'Uncle' or 'Aunty' out of respect. Never by their name alone.

Uncle Kishore displayed a bulging lump on his left cheek. Blood trickled down his face as he wearily stumbled in, steadying himself on surrounding vehicles. He was a short stocky man in his late forties with two boys, around the same age as my brother Aziz and me. Uncle

Kishore lost his wife five years ago to tuberculosis. It had hit him hard, yet he never failed to put on his mask and play the joker in the crowd. His sense of humour carried him through the toughest of times. Around the time he lost his wife, he lost all his hair too. Except for the dwindling comb-over at the front. He still kept a special little plastic comb for it in his shirt pocket. It made me giggle every time he pulled it out to manage his frail tufts. I refrained from any jokes myself that day though. This was serious.

"Kishore, come here and take a seat," Adha said. Kishore hesitantly took a few painful steps forward, leaning his hand against a car for support, dragging his left leg behind him; his trousers torn and blood-stained.

"My goodness, what happened to you?" Adha asked, obviously deeply troubled by his appearance. Uncle Kishore lowered himself wearily on a wooden stool that Adha had hastily cleared for him, tossing his car jack to one side.

"Amin's soldiers," he muttered, squinting at the back of his hands.

We froze like statues. My jaw dropped. Before anyone noticed, I pursed my lips together like a folded hem.

"Did they do this to you?" one worker asked, his eyes wide as he scanned Uncle Kishore's injuries.

"I visited the bank to withdraw funds. With everything that's going on, I thought it was time I took out Nita's savings. She would have wanted our boys to use it for their future. The bank clerk kept looking over my shoulder whilst serving me and something didn't feel right. As I walked past the post office, three of Amin's soldiers pushed me into the alleyway. They beat me, called me Muhindi scum, and howled at me, exclaiming that my money belonged to them. They took everything. Everything!" he cried.

I'd never seen a grown man cry. He felt he'd lost the battle already. In reality though, it hadn't even begun.

"I can't afford to run this car or pay for any of its repairs. What's the use? They'll take it from me regardless. Do me a favour and sell it. Get anything you can for it. It's time to pack up and go."

Uncle Kishore's experience made us all realise the threat was real. Our worst fears had materialised in front of our eyes. It was high time we considered leaving Uganda.

When Adha and I got home that night, we found Maa frantically gathering suitcases.

"We have to go; we have to leave as soon as possible!" she blurted.

"Maa, calm down. What's happened?"

"Lata's son, Jai, was beaten today. He refused to surrender his wallet and car keys to a group of Amin's soldiers. So, they used brute force. The poor boy has ended up with a broken leg and seventeen stitches on the back of his head," she whimpered.

Adha and I glanced at each other, taking a deep breath.

"Can you believe some staff at the hospital were refusing to treat him? In the end, a kind doctor offered to help. What will I do if something happens to our family? I'll never forgive myself. We have to prepare now. We won't be safe until we leave," Maa cried.

The weight of uncertainty burdened our hearts. Our eyes brimmed with sorrow.

Our little blue settee caught my eye. The site of many siblings battles, family gatherings for TV nights and a source of comfort on days of sickness. The holes in the little green lampshade on the side table projected a mosaic pattern onto our uneven magnolia walls, which were bare except for a black-and-white photo of the Kaaba in Mecca; the only picture frame we had in the house.

Were we really going to leave our home behind? What about my dog, Rocky?

How would we handle this mammoth task and accept the situation for what it was?

Adha and I chose not to tell Maa about Uncle Kishore. We both stood motionless but robust, like grounded lighthouses, whilst Maa uncontrollably crashed around us gathering our belongings.

CHAPTER FOUR
1967 - Kakira, Uganda
Age 14

"Hold the bag open, Kimo. Stop acting like a scaredy-cat! You're fourteen, not four."

"I'm not scared, Miah. I just hate lizards."

Lizards petrified Kimo to his very core. Oddly enough, he was fine with snakes.

"Hurry, she'll be home soon," I moaned.

It had taken the best part of our day for me to catch the darn thing. I wasn't about to let my master plan fail. I'd trapped the lizard in my hands, my palms tightly cupped together. It tickled more than anything.

"On the count of three, Kimo. One, two, three!"

I plunged my hands, still holding the lizard, deep into the tatty potato sack. Kimo secured it with a knot. The little lizard was in place, darting about frantically to find an escape route. Next came phase two. We made our way over to my Aunt Maryam's place, only four doors down from my house. My Aunt Maryam was Maa's second cousin. She never failed to report my antics to my mother. She managed to acquire so much information about everyone in the village. She'd often bake cakes and make Mandazi for the neighbours, as an excuse to drop in on them for cups of chai and village gossip, as did many of the women. She would find out who was to marry whom and what their dowries were rumoured to be. Gossip was her only proper job, along with the occasional stirring of the wooden spoon in the kitchen. Surprise parties would be ruined. *"A slip of the tongue"*, she would claim, using her increasing age as her only excuse. There was no need for a radio station on our street. She would broadcast daily news without fail. That fine day, Aunt Maryam was busy at the outdoor markets, doing her weekly grocery run. Perfect circumstances for the perfect plan.

Crouched behind the back-garden wall, we had a full view of the kitchen and the main hallway. Our pathway was clear with not a soul in sight. Like bandits, we crept through the back door, with the lizard sack securely in hand. Kimo stayed on lookout duty whilst I sneaked into the kitchen.

I could see my aunt's large aluminium cooking pot standing by the side of the stove. Sparkling clean, it was ready for the evening's lentil dish. She liked to make lentils every Thursday. A fresh bowl of lentil stew, heavily garnished with coriander, would often make its way to our home by early evening.

After emptying the contents of the sack into her prized pot, I carefully replaced the lid.

"Now, we wait," I giggled.

An hour passed.

"How long? I need to pee," Kimo whimpered, squatting like a desperate toddler.

"Just wait. Perhaps she's running late today."

Puzzled by her absence, we wondered about the delay. Inky clouds had congregated, indicating an imminent storm.

"Someone will see us behind this wall. Let's move from here, Miah," Kimo pleaded, aware of the rain clouds that loomed above.

Most of the houses on our street were of similar dimensions. They all had a small uneven hallway that led from front to back. Either side of those hallways were compact rooms. Three bedrooms, a small kitchen area, a tiny bathroom, and a living room, which we labelled the *'TV room'*. Tiered corrugated iron sheets topped each home, offering an acoustic treat whenever it rained. Although most of these houses were conventionally small, like bungalows, they had spacious backyards that would stretch for at least twenty to thirty metres, leading towards thick pockets of trees and jungle landscapes.

"Kimo, this is the best spot. The kitchen is in plain view and I want to see what happens."

"What if your Uncle Ahmed opens the lid first? Then what will you do?" He shuddered.

I didn't want to think of that as a possibility. The outcome would be frightful.

"That won't happen. You need to be quiet, stop bouncing and just—"

A figure floated into the kitchen. It was my aunt.

"Perfect," I whispered.

We waited patiently for a moment as she delicately opened the bag of lentils, treating them as if they were a pouch filled with gems. She used a teacup to scoop for measurement. She finally reached for the lid of her pot.

"Here we go," I chuckled.

"Aagh!" She screamed so loud that her voice cracked. The teacup shattered on the tiled floor, spilling her carefully gathered grains. She took another breath immediately and screamed again, her cry as loud as a foghorn.

"Miah, that was worth it," Kimo gasped, struggling to contain his amusement as we sprinted away. My eyes streamed with tears of laughter as I ran ahead of him, my lips unable to spout any words.

Later that evening, after a fulfilling day of meandering with Kimo, I approached the front door of my home with extreme caution. Aunty Maryam could have alerted the entire village, my mother being first on the list. Everything looked calm and there was no sign of danger, Maa, or her death stare.

Upon entering, I slipped off my flip-flops in the hallway, clasped them in my hand and tiptoed towards my bedroom, ignoring the sound of Shafina and Kabir's muffled arguments as I passed. Reaching for my door handle, I carefully extended my arm.

"Amir!" came a chilling voice.

Inevitably, I turned around and observed Maa, standing with her slipper in her hand and wildfire in her eyes. That was it. I was finished.

"I know what you did. Mr Singh also saw you running with that rascal friend of yours," she fired, her words like shards of icicles being launched from an angry blizzard. "Don't bother pleading with me, telling me it wasn't you. Poor Maryam had the fright of her life. You should be ashamed of yourself. Why do you keep doing this to her?"

At this stage I realised denial wasn't an option. Even I couldn't tame this cyclone.

"Why does she keep telling you everything I get up to? She needs to stop gossiping," I roared. I was brave outside, but my soul was quivering like a hatchling.

Suddenly, her leather slipper launched past my head, missing my ear by a fraction, denting the paint work on my bedroom door. Maa was normally terrible at throwing, but that was a close shave.

"You will have NO dinner tonight. *That* is your punishment. Go in your room and don't show me your face 'til morning. Tomorrow, you'll apologise to your aunt."

"But Maa—"

"Go!"

Dangling on the edge of my bed, my stomach grumbled as I listened to the joyful sounds of my family having dinner. It was chicken karahi on the menu that night and I heard Adha compliment the cook. Although the compliments were directed at Maa, everyone knew it was Johari who was the main chef. She was originally from Kenya and had learned to create many Indian dishes. She was the leading workforce in the house and always joined us during mealtimes. On occasion, she would sneak bits of food to my room if she knew I was under strict punishment. I hoped she'd come to my rescue that night with something, but unfortunately, I heard her leave after dinner.

The churning of my empty stomach made me heave. My little brother, Kabir made his way to our room. His flip-flops had a very distinct sound, so I could always guess when he was about. He often pranced around like a merry horse.

"Why are you still awake? Maa told you to go to sleep,"

he said, stamping his hooves on the ground.

"She told me to go to my room without dinner. Not to go to sleep," I protested, resting my hands on the bed at either side of me. Kabir was usually civil with me. But if he ever found an opportunity to get me into trouble, he'd grab it like a lion latching on to a zebra's neck. Aziz and I bossed him around, so I guess it was payback for him.

He opened the bottom dresser drawer, which neatly housed his clothes and belongings. Reaching in, he took out a paper bag of sweets.

"I've got five left in here," he said slyly, before shovelling them all into his mouth at once. "And now I've got none," he scoffed, barely spitting out his words.

I'd surprised myself by generating an impromptu death stare.

"Go to sleep, little boy. I don't want your sweets."

"Well, you could have had dinner, it was delicious. Maa even made a sponge cake," he bragged, swinging his head left and right like a pendulum, hands firmly on his hips.

A cheap shot from Kabir, but it worked. I'd missed out on cake... cake!

"Even Mother Goose had some cake today, ha!" Kabir gibed.

Mother Goose was Kabir's pet hen, along with twenty other chickens he kept in a coop in the backyard. They were the light of his life. Johari had a son, Tito, seventeen years old, who would often come to the house and help us with outdoor work and general maintenance in exchange for weekly pocket money. However, most of the time he assisted Kabir in building and maintaining his chicken coop. At age nine, Kabir was an inquisitive boy.

He loved new projects and taking on fresh challenges. He dedicated much of his time to these sorts of things. Maa allowed the chickens under strict conditions; that they were to be Kabir's responsibility, and that the eggs be brought into our kitchen. Every evening, Kabir would grasp his little black flashlight and dash into the backyard, rounding up his friends into the coop for the night. He would count them one by one as they entered the coop, including Mother Goose, who was special enough to get a kiss and a cuddle. I couldn't make him understand that Mother Goose, in the well-known fairy tale, was a goose and not a chicken. He didn't want to take on board my suggestion of Sean Connery as a name. I'd finally had the chance to watch 'Dr No' at the cinema, without a ticket, and as a result, James Bond was my new obsession.

"How can you kiss Mother Goose goodnight, knowing that you just ate her cousin at the dinner table?" I mocked.

"Maa said those are different kinds of chickens she cooks. They're not real ones," he yelled.

"Of course. How could I forget?" I mumbled, smacking my lips.

Turning the other way, I fell asleep.

Deep hunger pangs jolted me back to reality a few hours later. The house was still, with an unusual coolness. I could hear Kabir snoring. Visions of cake plagued my mind. I pondered over whether Kabir's sweets would have kept me going until morning, or whether Johari would come back and sneak me a snack.

A tiny pebble came flying through the window, cracking against my bed post. *Could it be?*

I rushed over and saw Kimo standing outside.

"You want to come out, Miah?" he whispered.

"Yup! Let's go," I agreed, and without further ado, I climbed out with Kimo once again crouched down on his knees.

We scuttled around to the backyard. Nothing stirred in the still night air. Chirping crickets echoed into the black velvet sky. Uganda's peaceful nights were bliss, with every star on display like shimmering sequins on a bridal sari.

"Why do you keep sneaking out, Kimo? One of these days you'll get caught. We both will," I giggled.

"I couldn't sleep, Miah. You won't believe what happened today," Kimo responded in a melancholy tone. "Obote's soldiers landed on our street searching for any Africans who are not Ugandan. They searched our home and then we saw them do the same to our neighbours. They pulled African people out onto the street and beat them with bricks and bats."

"What? Why?" I shrilled.

"Well, I overheard my parents talking about Obote's soldiers. It's not good. They are driving out Africans from neighbouring countries back to where they came from. They're showing no mercy to men. Asians are safe, for now I guess," Kimo shrugged, whilst rubbing his belly.

The sheer thought was disturbing, however part of me didn't wish to believe it.

"What's the matter, Kimo?" I moaned, noticing his loss of concentration.

"I'm hungry!" he said, rubbing his belly again.

"I know the feeling. I'm starving. Maa sent me to sleep with no food. They had chicken karahi and cake tonight. Come on, let's get some food."

We edged towards the back door, but Maa had locked it from inside. We could have gone through my bedroom window, but Maa was a light sleeper and she would have caught us.

The look in Kimo's eyes changed. I recognised his expression as the one that always appeared before a catastrophic idea; one that almost always landed me in trouble.

"You want chicken, Miah? I'll get you chicken," he chortled, looking over my shoulder at Kabir's chicken coop.

"No way! Adha will murder me. We can't," I bleated, condemning the sheer idea of it.

"Miah, I'm hungry, come on. Is he really going to notice if one little chicken goes missing? He has fifty of them!"

"Twenty-one to be precise, he counts them every night. So yes, he will notice and it's me who will get the blame."

Almost immediately, I began questioning whether he would potentially notice or not. *Maybe I could say a Hyena ate it, or that it escaped?* All I knew was that I was hungry, and I couldn't bear it anymore.

My single deep sigh was a signal to Kimo that I was on board.

"One little chicken, Kimo. Just one."

It didn't take us long to seize one of Kabir's feathered friends, making sure not to grab Mother Goose. If his prized madam was taken, the world would know about it. The temptation was there though, believe me.

A little further beyond where our yard ended, was a derelict spot with plenty of broken branches and sticks to create a makeshift barbeque. We gathered what we could and slowly roasted our catch over a warm fire. Kabir's little chicken tasted like a piece of heaven.

"Burp!"

"Kimo that's disgusting," I giggled.

"But so good, right, Miah?"

"Yes, absolutely."

The night was ours, speckled with stars. Kimo jumped to his feet and pointed to a fiery shooting star.

"You know, my sister says, if you see a shooting star, you should make a wish," he said, gazing up at the sky.

"You really believe what girls say about that sort of thing? It's nonsense," I teased, wiping my mouth with the inside of my pyjama top.

"If it's true, Miah, my wish is that we always stay together as brothers." He smiled.

Kimo had a marshmallow core in contrast to his spiky madness. I could see a lot of my own personality within him. At times it felt as if my increasingly daring nature was a result of my friendship with Kimo.

"I think that chicken's got to your head," I joked.

We sneaked back into our homes before the dawn's orange hues appeared. Standing on my tiptoes, I saw Kabir fast asleep, snoring away on the top bunk. Tightly pressing my hand over my mouth, I tried my best to avoid chuckling. I had an odd feeling of guilt. But no regrets.

CHAPTER FIVE

4th October 1972 - Kakira, Uganda
Age 19

Amin's deadline was looming with only 4 weeks remaining. We had begun preparations to obtain our passports. The only place that could issue them was the British High Commission office in Kampala. Many families were making the three-hour journey on coaches and minibuses to stand in lengthy queues outside the office. Hundreds of Asians were waiting patiently every day, sleeping on the streets, desperate to receive their passports before the expulsion period. Canada had started the ball rolling by offering to take in refugees. Britain, Italy, the USA, Denmark and many others soon followed, finally offering sanctuary to thousands of Ugandan Asians in limbo, desperate to flee Amin's regime. Many had hastily departed.

"I'm sure I had a copy, I just can't find it," Maa yelled, dumping the contents of her bedroom drawers on the floor.

"Maa what are you looking for? Why did you ask Johari to wake me up so early?" I asked, pressing my knuckles into my eyes. She looked deeply troubled. Papers were scattered everywhere with no trace of her usual obsessive cleaning habits.

"Amir I can't find your—"

"It's fine, Jilu. Don't panic. I've sorted it. Mahesh is going to Jinja next week and he'll get a copy of the birth certificate," Adha chimed in, catching his breath as he rushed in from the hallway.

"What!? You don't have my birth certificate?" I shrieked.

"Mahesh is one of our most reliable friends. Honestly, we're blessed. Ever since we moved to Kakira, he has been like a saviour, supporting us through thick and thin," Maa was singing his praises, oblivious of me.

"Amir, we're not sure if we misplaced it after we moved from Iganga, but it's nothing to worry about. It just means there will be a delay in receiving your passport. We need to leave today as planned to Kampala to sort the rest of the passports. I've made arrangements for you too. Everything is in place. We can discuss this on our journey," Adha said firmly. "Tell Aziz to get ready. We should leave now if we want to catch the eight o'clock bus," he explained, packing his shoulder bag with documents, cash and some snacks Maa had prepared for our early morning trip.

Initially, I wanted to explode, seething with anger. I steadied myself upon noticing the stress-ridden faces of both my parents. They just wanted to do what was physically possible day by day to get us out. Composing myself, I took a deep breath and forced my worries to the back of my mind.

"Don't forget to feed Rocky, Maa!" I grunted as we left

the house.

"What's wrong with you today? Too early for you, sloth?" Aziz enquired with a snigger.

"Why would you care," I yelled.

Adha marched in military form to the bus stand, only a few minutes away from our home. Aziz and I tried to keep up, like shabby trainee recruits. Maa had slipped me an extra tiffin of food in my satchel as I left. She always over packed and fussed over us. I couldn't help but wonder what delights were ready for us to devour in that little capsule of paradise. We were expecting to be back the same evening, all being well. Knowing how long the journey would be, I'd brought along a pillow to rest my head on the bus. It was too early for me to function and I was too tired to worry about things beyond my control.

When we finally boarded our bus, there were barely any seats left. We luckily got the last few seats at the front, otherwise it would have been a two hour wait for the next coach. We settled down and I was out like a light within minutes. Even after our change over at Jinja, I drifted off again quite readily.

"Wake up, Amir!" Aziz hissed, thrusting his elbow into my rib cage.

"Stop attacking my chest. You know about my ribs," I yelled, following up with a humongous yawn and super long stretch.

"Come on, get up! You've been snoring like a tractor all the way here. We have to go, you teenage sloth!" Aziz complained, pulling me by my arms in his hurry.

"Ok, ok, I'm moving. Don't manhandle me."

Passengers disembarked as if money showered down from the skies, pushing and shoving.

Adha belted from outside the coach doors, "Boys, come on, we have to join the queue, be quick. I can see it all the way up the high street. Move it, move it!"

We grabbed our belongings and headed towards the British High Commission office. Crowds hastily migrated in the same direction, shoulder to shoulder like soldiers.

We could see that the queue had extended to boundless lengths. Weary men waited in line with odd pockets of exhausted women, struggling with their distressed children.

"This is ridiculous Adha. We will be here all night at this rate," I complained, scrutinising the queue.

Three hours later, we were hungry, thirsty, and snappy. Our bodies drenched in sweat; we were ready to drop on the scorching pavement.

"Ok, boys. We'll take it in turns to stand here now, two at a time. Meanwhile, one of us can head across the road and rest under the canopies of the high street shops. We can swap every hour," Adha suggested. He acknowledged our struggles but was determined not to lose our place in the queue.

Turning behind me, I scanned the next family waiting in line. There was a young man, and his wife, standing patiently. She was clutching a young toddler, maybe twelve to eighteen months old at the most. They were sheltering under a yellow umbrella. I could see vulnerability and uncertainty in their eyes. The couple nodded in acknowledgement and gave me a friendly smile. It took me a moment before I realised I was staring and quickly averted my gaze after nodding back.

Aziz decided it was his turn to rest first, as I'd slept on the bus. He took my pillow and headed off towards the shops. We could still see him from our place in the queue. Many people had gathered to rest under the canopies. Some were fast asleep on their belongings; others were having something to eat. The stores were empty shells, no longer trading, with countertops covered in dust. The tailor shop, the shoe shop, the fashion store, the grocery store; they all had Asian proprietors. It had once been a haven for family outings and shopping trips; the shoe shop in particular was my favourite. An elderly Indian gentleman who owned the store would make a sweet appear from behind my ear. He was the one who inspired me to learn magic tricks and the art of illusion. We'd often visit Kampala at weekends and spend the entire day shopping, eating, playing in the park, and then concluding with an evening showing of the latest Bollywood release at the Odeon cinema. But alas—it had become a ghost town.

An hour later we weren't much closer. The rumbling of my gut gave me my lunchtime signal. Adha and I began tucking in to Maa's onion bhajis. It was times like these that we really appreciated the fuss she would make. I offered some to the couple behind us, and their little one rewarded me with a beaming smile.

Adha's eyes had become heavy.
"Adha why don't you swap with Aziz? I'll stay here."
He reluctantly nodded in agreement and made his way to the canopies.

We carried on this way, swapping and changing through the duration of the day. The agonising wait was taking its toll on the poor child behind us. I could see he was fatigued as his mother blotted his little tears with her scarf.

It was approaching six o'clock in the evening and the office was due to close. However, we were only two places away from being served at the kiosk inside the building and being within the building itself gave us some hope of being seen in time. My eyes were drawn periodically to the worn-down carpet beneath us, which had distinct triangular patterns still visible despite the wear and tear. In order to pass time on our last leg, I began counting how many triangles were left to cross until we reached the desk.

We only had 4 triangles to go, before a member of staff burst out of a side door. He announced that the office would be closing for the night and reopening again at eight o'clock the following morning.

"You can't do that!" I cried out. Scanning the room, I realised everyone's gaze was upon me.

"Amir, calm down," Adha exclaimed, embarrassed, but also just as annoyed. The crowd followed suit, yelling at the officials. Angered, frustrated, and upset. We were truly disappointed, being so close.

Many families took shelter that evening under the canopies and other surrounding areas. Some headed off to local cafes for food and snacks. Huddled under the canopy of the deserted shoe shop, I thought about the owner. *Where is he now? Could he have already left the country with his family? Was he allowed to take any of his lovely shoes? Who will run the store now?*

"Come on boys, let's go!" Adha said, dusting down his brown checked trousers.

"Where are we going?" Aziz asked.

"Odeon cinema is a ten-minute walk. Let's watch a movie and get something to eat," Adha replied, smiling.

Aziz and I bounced to our feet.

Would this be the last movie we watch here in Uganda? I wondered. I was secretly hoping we would watch Rajesh Khanna's movie 'Apna Desh'—and we did.

Rajesh Khanna had a medicinal effect on his audience that night. His on-screen presence transported us to a world where justice prevailed and good defeated evil, all because a hero took charge. After making a mental note of the hero's salmon shirt with oversized collars and of his slick hairstyle, I pondered over genuine heroes.

Did anyone exist powerful enough to stand up against Amin's outrageous commands? Would a mighty hero survive crocodiles? Maybe heroes don't get a taste of victory in reality... do they? Perhaps that's why we have cinemas, to help us forget that the world can be a cruel place.

Adha and Aziz slept through most of the movie, enjoying the air-conditioned hall after indulging on snacks. Mesmerised by Rajesh Khanna, I couldn't possibly have fallen asleep. Bollywood delivered a few hours of contentment, but like all marvellous things, it wasn't long before the escapism came to an abrupt end.

Somewhat rejuvenated, we headed back to the deserted shoe shop to rest. It was a matter of hours before we'd have to join the queue again.

"Take my pillow, Adha, I'll stay up for now. I'm not

sleepy anymore." I smiled.

The next morning, we once again made our way to the queues, three hours before opening time. We didn't expect to see anybody there so early, but crowds had already emerged. Thankfully, we were seen within an hour of opening and got passports issued for Maa, Adha, Kabir and Shafina. My siblings had their names on my parents' passports. Aziz was lucky. He had his paperwork from the previous year, having been to India to study. That left just me.

Adha finally spoke of his plans for my proposed departure. He explained that they'd all be leaving Uganda soon and I'd be travelling back to Kampala alone to have my passport issued.

"I can't believe I have to come back to Kampala on my own," I protested, as we boarded the lunchtime bus back home.

"Maybe Amin's soldiers should recruit you here instead. They could use a sloth like you," Aziz gibed. I ignored him.

"Look, Amir, it's nothing to worry about. As soon as you have your birth certificate, you need to have your health check and smallpox vaccination. Uncle Mahesh will take you in his car to the clinic. Once that's complete, you'll come back here and get your passport issued. Uncle Mahesh will also take you to Entebbe airport. You'll be fine," Adha reassured me.

"But I'll be alone, Adha. You'll all be leaving in a couple of days," I said, thoroughly disappointed.

"You won't be alone, Amir. Your Uncle Usman will be here with you. He's also staying behind to ensure his paperwork is issued in time. He's in the same situation,"

Adha reassured me again.

Uncle Usman was my mum's younger brother. He had a wife and four children staying with extended family in Kenya. He barely spoke, as his lips seldom left his smoking pipe.

"Amir, I don't want to panic your mother, but it's important that I get our women out of Uganda as soon as possible. Amin's soldiers are ruthless and stories of their atrocities against women are disturbing."
We both fell silent.

As we travelled back home to Kakira that day, anxiety churned in my empty stomach. *What if I don't get my birth certificate? What if my passport isn't issued in time? Will Amin's soldiers kill me? Will I ever make it out of here alive?*
I knew I had to take heed of my father's every instruction. There was no choice.

It overjoyed Maa to see us back home. I could tell she had been worried sick in our absence.
"Thank God you're all safe and sound," she yelled, whilst grabbing hold of us, one at a time squeezing our heads between her flour covered palms. "You must be hungry, come eat some rotis," she said, clapping the excess flour off her hands.
"Maa we managed just fine. The queue was so long, we had to sleep under the high street canopies. They saw to us this morning in the office and everything is ready," I said, following her into the kitchen.

"Thank goodness it's done," she said with an enormous sigh of relief.

I could see her relief was short-lived as Adha spoke again.

"We leave tomorrow, Jilu. We have to go. I've arranged for Amir to travel out of Uganda with Usman. Mahesh will keep an eye on him until his paperwork is complete."

"What utter nonsense! I'm not leaving my child here. If we go, we go together, otherwise we don't leave at all," she cried.

"JILU! Listen to me!" Adha stormed, his voice almost shattering.

The last time I heard Adha yell like that, I was six years old and had tried to wash a car at the garage with pumice stone.

We all froze. His voice immediately softened.

"Look. If we don't leave now, it may become more difficult for us to leave later with our belongings. Lately they've become more and more strict at the airports. You'll need your sewing machine. I'll need some tools from the garage, and we need to take some basics from the house where possible. We are starting from scratch in an unknown land, so we need to survive somehow. I've thought and planned this through a thousand times in my head. Amir will be fine. He's my son too. But he's also a grown man, Jilu," he said, placing his hands on both her shoulders. He turned to look at me. His eyes projected confidence.

"He's not a little child. He can do this," he said with a proud smile.

Knowing that I had my Uncle Usman staying behind with me, gave me strength. But I was still riddled with the heartache of knowing that I would be parting with my family within a matter of hours. As annoying as my siblings were at times, I loved them dearly and couldn't imagine life without them.

CHAPTER SIX
1967 - Kakira, Uganda
Age 14

I had a small gang of school friends and we would often make plans to go to the cinema, also known as the recreation club, in Kakira. We rarely paid for our tickets. We would sneak past good old Omari, who was the usher on duty most days. Omari was possibly in his late sixties. Rumoured to have taken a vow of celibacy since finding Christianity, he liked to volunteer at the centre, tucking into snacks and reading the daily delights of the Uganda Argus. Whilst on duty, he would be casually dressed in a pair of shorts, flip-flops, and an oversized white t-shirt, along with a super bright flashlight which he hung around his neck on a long brown cord.

A screening of the Bollywood movie 'An evening in Paris' starring one of my all-time favourite heroes, Shammi Kapoor, would be showing in the cinema.

"Ok, are we ready guys?" Harman said, clutching a handful of firecrackers, as he huddled behind a wall with the rest of us.

Tickets had sold out, and the film had already begun.

"Harman," I whispered. "Now might be a good time. Look! Omari's busy talking to the ticket clerk. Get ready to light them," I ordered, examining our surroundings, as Kimo and Niraj both crouched behind us.

Our eyes firmly fixed on the entrance, Harman lit his

Diwali leftovers and launched them immediately into the centre of the main doors.

Omari dived behind the booth, and the nervous ticket clerk ducked under his counter. This was our moment—so we ran.

Omari had caught sight of us dashing inside the cinema hall as he was lying on the floor. He realised he'd been hoodwinked, and chased after us, shouting Swahili slurs. We all entered the hall a few seconds apart from one another. I was last in. It was pitch black and not much was visible apart from the soft light of the projector, beaming onto the enormous screen.

"Miah! Here, here," came Kimo's voice. I glanced over to my right, only to catch sight of my brother Aziz sitting with his friends, looking unamused. Kimo bobbed his head up from in front of them like a jack-in-a-box, flapping his arms to get my attention. Joining Kimo, I took refuge near their feet, only to find Harman and Niraj also taking cover. We huddled together, giggling.

Aziz gave me a sharp clip round the head.

"You'll get caught one of these days," he whispered in frustration.

We couldn't help but gloat over our latest triumph. Omari came in with his flashlight but had no luck in locating us, as always. That evening we were on top of the world. The movie was amazing! The fight scenes, the music, the outfits. I felt like I'd starred in the film myself; a victorious hero.

Upon entering my home that night, my triumph fizzled into dust. I'd gone from being King of the Jungle to a tiny helpless mouse.

Kabir was standing in the living room shining his

chicken flashlight in my face. I'd had enough of darn flashlights that night. He was frowning so hard his eyebrows almost touched the tip of his nose. By his side was Maa with her hands firmly on her hips, her eyes peppered with suspicion. My father was sitting on the settee, catching up on news reports.

"Adha, he's here now. It's question time," Kabir bellowed, switching off his flashlight.

My father stood up and paced towards me. He cleared his throat and paused for a second before speaking.

"Amir, do you know where Kabir's chicken might be? He's counted them this evening and one seems to have gone missing. Kabir thinks you may have something to do with this. Do you know anything about this?" he asked calmly.

Hesitant about what to say, a scenario played in my mind where I looked Kabir square in the face, and told him I'd chopped, roasted, and digested his silly chicken the night before.

Knowing that Maa was scrutinising my body language, I stayed silent and exercised my best poker face.

"I sent you to bed last night with no chicken karahi. I hope you didn't get any ideas in the middle of the night," Maa probed, still firmly clasping her hips.

"What? Are you sure you've counted properly? And why would I do such a thing? That's crazy," I gasped, making sure not to lock eyes with Maa for too long.

"It was him, Maa, I know he's done something. Sooner or later, I'll prove it," Kabir yelled.

Adha gave me a nod, which was the official sign for *'you may leave now'*. Phew!

I gave Kabir a cheeky wink before heading off to my room. This roiled him up, leading to a scolding from both of our parents.

The next day, Harman, Niraj, Kimo and I went for a stroll to find some jambu trees.

"Oh my God, so they still don't know who took the chicken?" Niraj chuckled.

"Nah, they couldn't prove it was me. My brother is convinced that I took it or sold it. If only he knew," I said.

"Next time make sure you invite us for the barbeque." Harman laughed.

We all giggled for a few minutes until Niraj stopped us in our tracks.

"Look guys," he said, pointing up at the tree beside us.

It was brimming with the ripest, juiciest looking jambus we'd ever seen.

"I'm not going up there. Look." Kimo pointed to an ominous shadow, deep within the tree.

We moved towards the trunk to investigate.

"Erm, that's a Hornet's nest guys. I'm not climbing up there," I said, wide eyed, perfectly aware of the dangers.

"I think we should keep clear guys," said Kimo, stepping a few paces back.

Niraj and Harman were adamant that nothing would happen. They both volunteered to climb up there, just to prove that it was safe after laughing at our hesitance.

They carefully made their way up, deep into the tree, all the while making sure their movements didn't upset the nest.

"Get ready to catch guys," shouted Niraj.

He began throwing a few jambus down for us to gather. The first few were luscious. The next few had bites taken out of them.

Kimo and I looked up at them both in confusion. We

could see them giggling at one another, taking bites out of the jambus and then thrusting them down at us.

"Why those cheeky little—" Kimo muttered in frustration.

Revenge was already on my mind, but I could only think of one horrid plan. A wicked grin swept across my face.

After examining my surroundings, I found my usual weapon of choice, a trusty sugarcane rod. Aiming directly for the Hornet's nest, I gave it my best shot.

"Score!" I shouted with a triumphant smile.

Angry Hornets began descending from their little kingdom. The sheer look of horror in Harman and Niraj's eyes was worth a million shillings. Struggling to contain my laughter, Kimo and I couldn't stand there any longer. It was time to run.

As we sprinted back towards our homes, we glanced at each other, our eyes once again streaming from fits of laughter. We didn't even stop to check if they'd made it out of the tree. We carried on running till we reached my house, and then slowly tiptoed into my backyard. We sat and laughed for hours that day. Kimo pulled out a handful of jambus he'd stuffed into his pocket. I'll never forget how good they tasted.

CHAPTER SEVEN

6th October 1972 - Kakira, Uganda
Age 19

"Bring it over here, Tito, there's still room," Adha shouted, wiping the sweat from his forehead, his eyes swollen and distressed.

Tito struggled with a humongous cardboard box, which towered over his head. It was generously taped on all sides except for the top which flapped open. He rested it next to the taxi, scratching his head, as if he was trying to figure out how everything was going to fit.

"The top isn't sealed; shouldn't we see to that now before we leave?" Maa asked, struggling to manage all the hand luggage.

"No, Jilu, we need to leave it accessible. They'll be reopening everything we own at the airport security desks. I'll take some extra tape to seal it properly after we pass our checks," Adha said, shoving the box into the back of the taxi. Tito stood; his head tilted to one side as he continued to scratch it.

Uncle Usman brought out another enormous suitcase from the house.

"I hope they let you keep all this luggage, Ismail. I've heard they're charging bribes to let you hold on to even minimal belongings," he said, as he hauled the case.

It was rare for me to hear Adha being called by his

first name. It felt comforting that day.

"It's true," Adha said. "They're charging bribes at every step in Entebbe. Bribes so you can keep your dignity. It makes me sick! How can Amin just strip us from the land we love? How can he just take away our lives like this?" Adha's expression changed. He'd been calm for weeks, and I knew he was trying to remain strong and level-headed for the rest of the family.

He dropped to his knees and placed both his hands on the ground.

"This is my soil. Uganda is my home, and now, I'll never see it again. I'll never see this house again, my blood, sweat and tears. All because Amin doesn't like the colour of my skin," he yelled.

My siblings froze.

I crouched down next to him and put my arm around his shoulders.

"Adha, don't worry, we will start again, and we will do what we do best. We will work hard, we will support each other as a family, and we will love our new home. We'll be just fine," I said, desperate to lift his spirits. This wasn't how I'd pictured our goodbyes.

Adha smiled faintly and pursed his lips together before shaking his head.

"My son is talking about working hard," he said, raising his eyebrows. He held me tightly in his arms as a few tears fell from his eyes.

Saying goodbye to Aziz, Kabir and Shafina was harder than I thought it would be. They'd each become very emotional when they squeezed into the back of the vehicle. Kabir and Shafina were both still so young and the fear of leaving, along with seeing Adha get so upset, had evidently upset them. I stood leaning into the open window, looking at their frightened faces. I explained that they needed to stay calm for Maa and Adha. Aziz also reassured them that everything would be ok.

"What if we don't see you again?" Shafina cried, blotting her tears with the end of her pink scarf.

"Not possible. I'm Rajesh Khanna! Invincible," I joked, coaxing a smile out of her.

Deep down though, the same worries were eating me up. *Would I ever see them again?*

"Amir, we are leaving now. You know what you have to do as soon as Mahesh brings your birth certificate. If he doesn't bring it by Thursday, you must go to Jinja yourself and get a copy as soon as possible. Don't you wait longer than that," Adha instructed. I continued nodding in acknowledgement, realising that this was really happening. They were leaving. A wave of pins and needles jolted through my arms and legs.

"I've left you some British pounds and some shillings too. You'll be permitted to take a maximum of fifty pounds out of the country. Use the rest of the money for food, travel and save some shillings to make sure you keep hold of your belongings at airport security. Your Uncle Usman will stay here with you, ok?"

"Yes, Adha," I said, lifting my head trying to appear confident, but deeply wounded by the grief of parting.

"We will be together again, Adha, don't worry about me. I've got this," I whispered, as I hugged Adha tightly, and prayed it wouldn't be for the last time.

"Eat properly, Amir. I've left plenty of food in the kitchen for both you and your Uncle," Maa said, her voice quivering. She didn't last for another second before she burst into tears. We embraced. I continued to reassure her that I would be fine, and that it would be a matter of days before we would be reunited.

Maa sat in the car sobbing into her shawl, unable to say any more. We waved goodbye to one another as the taxi slowly pulled away.

"Kabir!" I shouted.

My brother hung his head out of the window.

"I'm sorry I ate your chicken!" I said with a cheeky grin.

"Wait—what chicken?... Oh my God, no way! Ha ha. It's been five years! I knew it was you," he chuckled, smiling back at me as the taxi drove further and further away into the distance.

CHAPTER EIGHT
1967 - Kakira, Uganda
Age 14

"Maa... Maa!"

"Amir, what on earth is wrong?" Maa shrieked. Startled by my outburst, she'd almost dropped one of her prized teacups. She caught it within the towel she was using to dry it.

"Amir, what's happened?" she asked. "You almost made me drop that."

Struggling to catch my breath, my lungs were closing up, the passage of oxygen restricted by sheer terror. She looked deep into my pupils and her expression changed.

"Amir, you don't look so good. Tell me, what is it?" she pleaded.

"Maa where is Johari? Where is Tito? We have to hide them, now!" I managed to gasp out, my voice trembling.

"What? Why? Johari has gone to Kenya to visit her sister. You already know this. She won't be back for a few weeks."

"And where is Tito, Maa?"

"He's in the backyard with Kabir fitting a new lock on his chicken coop. What's going on? Why do we have to hide him?"

"Maa, Obote's soldiers are checking everyone's houses for any Africans who are not Ugandan. If they have no tax card, they'll beat them in the streets, take them away and kill them," I yelled.

"What? How can they do that? Surely they have no right to—"

"Kimo told me it happened on his street too, Maa. There's no time for this. We have to hide him now."

Bursting through the back door, I sprinted towards Tito and Kabir. Kabir stood holding the door of the chicken coop in place, while Tito was using a screwdriver to fit some new bolts.

"Tito, they will take you away. Come in the house now and hide under my bed," I cried, pulling him by his arm. He'd dropped his tools. He understood the danger and followed me without any hesitation.

"Who will take him away?" Kabir shouted as we were heading back to the house.

"Obote's soldiers," I yelled, glancing back at him. Kabir's face turned pale. He ran behind us.

We shoved Tito into our bedroom and helped him slide underneath our bunk bed. On top of our wardrobe we had a suitcase that we used to store old books. It was heavy, and we pulled it down, with difficulty, and slid it under the bed. We tried to block any sight of Tito hiding there. We stuffed whatever we could lay our hands on to fill the gaps.

"Tito are you ok?" I whispered.

"Yes, I'm fine, Amiri," he muttered.

Many Africans couldn't pronounce my name. They would call me Amiri instead of Amir. I quite liked it! Had quite a fun ring to it.

There was a pounding on the front door. We had a little knocker attached to the door, but the soldiers didn't use it. Adha and Aziz were at the garage and Shafina was at a birthday party. Cautiously, I made my way to the door, as I couldn't possibly let Maa or Kabir answer it.

The thumping continued until I plucked up the courage to open the door. There were three soldiers standing in their khaki uniforms. The one in the middle was holding his gun up. It looked like he'd used the butt of his rifle to strike our door.

"Where is your father or mother, boy? Do you have any workers here?" he asked sharply.

Another one stepped forward, "Who else lives in this house with you?"

"Just my two brothers, my sister and my parents. Why do you ask?" I muttered, trying to appear innocent.

My initial reaction would have been to reach into my back pocket, pull out my catapult and fire sharp rocks into their faces. But I knew I was no match for their rifles. They pushed past me and stormed into our home.

Maa rushed forward.

"Why are you in my house? What right do you have to enter my home?" she exclaimed.

"We have every right to be here. We are under strict orders from our government and our leader, Milton Obote, to search for non-Ugandan residents without tax cards. No tax card, no rights. Understood?"

Maa stood there, her mouth hanging open. I'd never witnessed her so speechless before.

They ransacked the house, combing all the rooms, along with the backyard. They'd opened Maa's wardrobe. At that point I became nervous, hoping they wouldn't search under my bed. A soldier then moved steadily into my room, while a hollow feeling overcame me, and my limbs felt numb. Haziness engulfed my body, with black spots appearing before my eyes. The catapult in my back pocket crossed my mind again. A stale scent of gunpowder lingered in the air.

He walked out and nodded to the other soldiers. "Nothing here," he said.

A silent sigh left my lips. Although I could now feel my limbs, they'd turned limp and jelly-like.

The soldiers left with no further questions and made their way towards neighbouring houses. Maa insisted that we waited at least an hour before we got Tito out of hiding. During that grueling wait, we could still hear the soldiers on our street, banging on doors, screams and cries. I was praying and hoping none of the neighbours would mention anything about Tito being here. They all knew him.

After a long wait, Maa came dashing back from the window.

"They've gone", she said, as the colour flowed back into her cheeks.

"Thank you all for saving my life," Tito said, embracing Maa.

"Don't worry, son. We will keep you safe as long as you are with us, Tito," Maa said, hugging him back.

"Tito. We'll never let them touch you. Don't worry," I said, giving him a high-five.

I'll never forget the look of terror on his face that day. It was the first time I began to question why people hurt others because of their differences, and why humans kill one another over labels imposed by society.

CHAPTER NINE
===

1969 - Kakira, Uganda
Age 16

The street was lined either side with flickering Ugandan flags. Most of the people from our village had been gathered near the oil mill for over an hour, eagerly awaiting the arrival of the President in the midday sun.

Clutching my autograph book, I patiently stood waiting for the convoy to arrive.

"Kimo, he'll be arriving any minute. You've dared me. Now watch me do it!" I chirped; excited with a hint of nervousness.

"Miah, there's too many people and he'll have so much security around him. You'll never get Milton Obote's autograph. We're too far back over here," Kimo said, smirking.

An initial low humming transformed into loud cheering.

"Kimo look! He's here," I said, stretching tall on my tiptoes to see beyond the gathering. An open top army jeep rolled into view, with General Idi Amin behind the wheel, waving to his fans. With his navy-blue cap tilted to one side and his medals glistening on display, he smiled as he led another vehicle into sight.

"Look! He's in that black Rolls Royce, Kimo," I said. "I'm going now, before I lose my chance."

"What! Miah, you can't. Look at all the soldiers in the jeeps behind him. Look at the size of Amin!" he yelled, as I bolted forward.

I battled through with all my might, pushing through the sea of bodies; all shoving each other to catch a glimpse of the President. As I elbowed my way to the front, I struggled to breathe amidst the cloud of body odour, clinging to every breath I inhaled. Bursting out into a clearing, I found myself just a few feet away from Obote's car. His driver opened the back door and I saw a gleaming black leather shoe peeking out from the edge. Milton Obote stepped out from his vehicle; the crowds cheered louder, waving their flags even higher. I took a deep breath and advanced towards him, one hesitant step at a time. Suddenly, an arm extended in front of me, like a large barrier blocking traffic. I looked up in horror to find General Amin staring down at me. His smile from earlier had evaporated and his pupils were fully dilated, staring directly into mine. I wanted to blink, but even my eyelids had frozen over.

"Let him through, General," came a gentle voice.

Amin and I both turned around to find Milton Obote beckoning for me to come forward. Amin immediately withdrew his arm and stepped aside.

"Go, boy, make it quick," he said sternly. His pupils were still wide and locked on me.

Air filled my lungs again and I proceeded towards the President, who was standing tall, giving me a warm smile. As I approached him, he pointed towards my autograph book.

"Would you like me to sign that for you, young man?" he asked kindly.

"Yes please, Sir," I said, handing him the book, my

hands trembling.

As he flicked through the pages and signed his name, I studied his face. He had a calmness about him. His eyes projected warmth. I'd previously seen what his soldiers were capable of, so I was still very much afraid him.

He handed my book back and patted me on the head.

"There you are, young man," he said with a smile, before moving forward to greet everyone.

Without further ado, I quickly immersed myself into the crowds, eager to avoid eye contact with General Amin. I felt as if there was something most unsettling about him. I never wanted to find myself in his presence ever again.

CHAPTER TEN

12th October 1972 - Kakira, Uganda
Age 19

Most Ugandan Asians had departed from Uganda, along with my family. Rocky and Uncle Usman were all I had left here. Pacing up and down the backyard, I devoted some time to Rocky.

"Fetch," I shouted, tossing a stick towards him.

Rocky was always ready for play. At eighteen months old, he was still a puppy, but he could bulldoze a crowd in seconds. He could brighten up anyone's day with the amount of love and energy he would exude. Maa had granted me permission to keep Rocky as a guard dog for our family home. But he'd turned out to be so loving towards strangers, that if a burglar ever broke into our home, he would have licked them to death before rolling over for a belly rub.

Rocky had the freedom to roam the full length of the backyard, and occasionally beyond. At night he slept in a very special eight by eight-foot kennel. It had a corrugated iron roof, just like our home. Tito and my dad worked incredibly hard to build it, pretty much over the same spot where Kabir used to have his old chicken coop. The 'chicken phase' novelty wore off after two years. Maa's prediction was correct, as she was inevitably lumbered with the upkeep. She eventually sold the chickens.

Some ended up on the dinner table with the help of our neighbour, who'd purchased and housed most of them, out of Kabir's sight. Maa always crafted her stories well to avoid Kabir's suspicions, but might as well have not bothered, as he'd lost interest and no longer cared.

Rocky was tired, and it was time for his mid-afternoon siesta. A single tear trickled down my dry, sun-drenched cheek. I was coming to terms with the fact that taking him with me wasn't an option. I'd have to plan for someone to offer him a home. The question was… who would I ask?

"Amir!", Uncle Usman yelled from the back door. "Come inside. Amin's on television."

My gut churned. *What was this evil man saying now? Could I put up with hearing anymore of the poison he was spewing?*

On the TV, an apprehensive looking journalist with a British accent was interviewing him. Amin's vast frame towered over the lean gentleman.

- "Actually, I took the decision for the economy of Uganda and I must make sure that every Ugandan gets the fruit of independence. Since independence actually, Uganda is not yet independent; I will say that. Even after the British handed over on the ninth of October 1962, Uganda is still not yet independent. Uganda will be independent after this! My decision! Afterwards, I want to see that the whole of Kampala's main street, is not full of Indians. It must be proper black administration in those shops, run by Ugandans."

I shook my head as Uncle Usman turned off the TV. In my opinion, there wasn't much difference between Amin and Hitler. Again, I wondered whether this was truly happening. *Would it all be a nightmare I'd be waking up from soon?*

A knock at the door transported me back to the room.

"Amir, marvellous news. I have your birth certificate. Here, keep it safe." Uncle Mahesh had arrived, thank goodness. This piece of paper would potentially save my life. I was so grateful he'd made it back when he'd promised he would.

"That's great news!" I said brightly. Briskly taking the paper from his hands, I'd noticed, although he'd had a successful trip, he looked awfully troubled.

"Are you ok? Come and sit down," I said, holding him by the arm and carefully guiding him over to the settee.

"Mahesh, what's the matter?" Uncle Usman asked.

He looked up and I could see the tension on his face.

"Look, I'll not hide anything or sugar-coat what I've seen in Jinja—it's not looking good. When I got there, I stopped by a lovely little cafe, no bigger than this living room, run by a small Asian family. I was just tucking into my samosas when some men stormed in and destroyed the place. They broke furniture and equipment. They pulled fixtures off the walls and terrorised the owners. That poor family was frightened. These men didn't quite resemble soldiers. Possibly just some local opportunists who couldn't wait until the deadline. Along with a few other customers in there, I was also asked to leave immediately. With no weapon to fight back, I did as I was told."

The pit of my stomach churned uncontrollably, like a water wheel rotating through swampy marshland.

"Why are they behaving like savages? Amin has created such a violent culture. How are we supposed to survive like this in our final days here?" I yelled.

Uncle Mahesh nodded and proceeded with the rest of the story.

"Eventually, the gang of men sent the Asian family out of the cafe with nothing but the clothes on their backs, slamming the door behind them. They stood there in silence, before the mother figure of the family burst into tears. We immediately hurried to their aid. They were told the business was no longer theirs and were warned never to return. A local customer seemed to know the family well and offered to drive them to their home. If I had a weapon or an opportunity, I would have fought back," Uncle Mahesh said, with his shoulders slumped.

"There's no point fighting back now. We have nothing left to fight for. It's a matter of days before they revoke our rights to everything here. Why fight over temporary assets?" Uncle Usman argued.

"Still. Ninety days should mean ninety days. This is vile behaviour. They have no regard for anything or anyone," Uncle Mahesh raged.

We sat for a moment, absorbing one another's words. Uncle Mahesh broke the silence.

"It's best if we now think about getting you to Jinja for your smallpox vaccination and health check, Amir. That's the next step. I also need to go for mine, so I'll take you in my car," he said, putting his hand on my shoulder.

I nodded back in agreement, as I tried to smile reassuringly.

"It will be Monday though. I have to drive some neighbours to the airport over the next few days—if the soldiers let me."

He let out a brief sigh before he carried on.

"It's up to you though, Amir. If you want to go to Jinja with me, you must wait. If you feel you can't wait, you could catch the bus tomorrow. It's just that I've promised your father that I would look out for you until you reach the airport safely. Jinja is becoming unstable," he said, obviously hoping I'd choose to go with him.

"It's not a problem. I'll wait," I said, wondering whether I'd live to regret my decision.

"Keep twenty shillings ready, they're taking bribes before they hand over the paperwork," Uncle Mahesh said, shaking his head in disgust.

CHAPTER ELEVEN

15th October 1972 - Kakira, Uganda
Age 19

Monday finally arrived. Uncle Usman seemed to cope well with the wait. For me, the days became stagnant. Even the clocks were reluctant to tick. My Uncle had been actively helping neighbours and other locals where possible, and many of them were returning the favour. Although we had enough money ourselves to leave Uganda, there were many who didn't have the funds to manage. We'd sold some items in the house to raise cash for those families who needed help. We gave Tito a tidy sum of money for him and his mother. Johari had left for Kenya once again, and Tito would follow suit after my departure. I kept urging him to leave as soon as he could, but he insisted on staying with us until we'd departed. Tito and I would routinely enjoy cups of masala chai together. We stood in the kitchen boiling the saucepan, attempting to speak.

"You know, I will miss you the most, Amiri."

"Tito, I'll miss you too, my brother. I just wish I could take you with me," I murmured, gazing down at the ground.

"Don't be silly. I can't live on tea and cake in Britain! I need ugali to survive."

Ugali was maize flour porridge and was Tito's favourite food. "I'll be happy and safe in Kenya with my family.

Don't worry about me," he giggled.

Although I smiled back at him, my facade was on the brink of collapse. The lump in my throat expanded. I wanted to speak but couldn't find the words. Tito must have sensed this as he immediately changed the subject.

"You know something? I always knew it was you who stole and ate Kabir's chicken when you were little?" he said with a smirk.

"What? Really? How?" I asked, feeling the lump in my throat recede.

"I was there when you were roasting it. I came to investigate the flames. Seeing you and Kimo there, slow-roasting Kabir's chicken, I knew you were up to no good."

Pouring our tea, Tito and I chuckled.

"We've made some great memories here, Tito. The good times will stay with me." I said, smiling at him.

"But you, Amiri, you were *too* naughty. You've changed, but still cheeky when you want to be," Tito said, grinning, exposing the gap between his two front teeth.

The honking of Uncle Mahesh's horn sounded outside. I opened the front door and spotted him waiting in his car with the windows down. He had a beautiful black Morris Minor, same as Adha's. He took great pleasure in polishing his car every week, buffing until he spotted his reflection. Shouting goodbye to Tito and Uncle Usman, I snatched my coat and headed out with a little apprehension.

The drive from Kakira to Jinja was short. Forty-five minutes, weaving through the trees on an uneven, narrow road. However, travelling with Uncle Mahesh felt like five minutes at the most. He was a married man, with a twelve-year-old daughter, Jaya. She was a gifted child, light-years ahead of her time both socially and academically. Uncle Mahesh supported her studies, as she was eager to pursue a career in the medical field. Despite being seven years her senior, there were times where I was intimidated by her conversations. I couldn't even pronounce the titles of her medical books, yet she would have her nose in them twenty-four hours a day. There was an unsettling aura about Jaya; I'd never truly seen her smile. In contrast, Uncle Mahesh was a jolly man. He'd always have a funny joke to crack and he enjoyed discussions about Bollywood movies and music. Everyone that knew him sought out his company. It left me wondering whether his daughter was an alien, or if she was perhaps adopted. Uncle Mahesh was a great friend of Adha's and was thoroughly respected in our village.

We listened to his radio all the way to Jinja. Elvis, Donny Osmond and The Beatles; they all transported us to another realm. A realm of fun, laughter and happiness.

As we approached Jinja, we noticed Amin's soldiers parading the streets in their vehicles, their guns at the ready. Their chilling presence made my hair stand on end.

We parked across the road from Jinja hospital and made our way to the clinic inside, attentive to our surroundings. The place had never been so busy. Staff were racing around giving out vaccinations and general health checks. Independent queues had formed, as people were desperate to obtain certificates as documented proof of having had their vaccines. After receiving our shots, Uncle Mahesh and I joined separate queues to see if we could identify a quicker route. However, we moved along at the same pace towards desks occupied by hospital clerks. Six white desks were stationed in a line, with staff working their way through the hordes of Ugandan Asians. Choosing to ignore the pacing gunmen, also scattered around the clinic, I stepped onto my tiptoes and peered towards the front, assessing the queue lengths. We continued for at least two hours amongst these noisy queues, my ears tuned into many people's stories of desperation like a radio dial; talk of having to leave behind pets, property, businesses, and friends. As I scanned the area, I witnessed families with young children, babies as young as a few days old being nursed under their mother's veils.

Uncle Mahesh was called forward by a clerk. Within seconds, I was also called to the next available desk.

Upon approaching the clerk, I observed him examining the room. He rolled his eyes at the queues and peered at everyone with disgust, as if discovering rotten fruit in his larder. He spotted me, frozen in front of him, fearful of his destructive glare. His large, compassionless eyes made me feel worthless; like gum stuck to the bottom of his shoes. His words had the same effect.

"You! Sit down and fill in this form," he ordered, his gaze still skewering me.

As I followed his instructions, he switched his attention back towards the crowds. I may as well have been invisible. Perhaps to him I was.

Handing him the completed form along with my birth certificate, I dared to make a little eye contact, twitching all the while. He snatched the papers from me.

I was no different from a prisoner, getting ready to go into a jail cell to carry out a life sentence. He took out a large blank certificate, filled my name in and stamped it using the hospital stamp and ink pad, neatly placed on his desk.

A sense of relief surged through me when the stamp pounded onto the piece of paper. One step closer to my family.

Reaching forward, I extended my arm towards the certificate, when the clerk swept it back from the edge of his desk.

"Money first," he grunted, subtly gesturing with his hands.

Opening my wallet wide, I took out twenty shillings.

He baulked at my contribution.

"No!" he sternly barked, "It is one hundred shillings."

"But I was told twenty shillings when I came in."

"How much do you have in your wallet, boy?" he asked, gesturing towards my hands.

It was then I realised I had made a rookie mistake.

"Only eighty-five," I quietly muttered, my mind questioning my honesty and stupidity.

"Ok, that will do. Give me that and take your certificate. If not, you leave with nothing. Do you understand, Muhindi? Hurry now, quietly put it in here," he said, carefully sliding open his bottom drawer.

There was no other option; I knew I'd lost this one. Feeling dehumanised and humiliated, I tossed the contents of my wallet into his drawer, took my documents, and left.

Uncle Mahesh was in reception waiting for me.

"All done, Amir?" he asked, rubbing his palms together.

"He took eighty-five shillings from me," I said, gazing down at the chequered patterns on the tiled floor

"What? Why? It should have been only twenty shillings," he blazed.

"It was my fault, Uncle. Not thinking, I opened my wallet in front of him and he saw what I had. It was too late."

"Oh, Amir. Ok. Never mind. Next time have some small notes ready, rolled up in your pockets. You may be faced with this again. Never, ever show your wallet or what you have," he said, letting out a deep sigh. "Come on, let's get you home."

The journey home had a different vibe. It was draining and interminable. Although Uncle Mahesh was his usual jolly self and was happily chatting away over the sound of Elvis' 'Jailhouse rock', I sat in silence most of the way home. The clerk had left me feeling deceived and violated. *Did my life have no value anymore? He openly called me a Muhindi.* We eventually passed by my old school. A gentle smile briefly swept across my cheeks as I recalled a few happy memories. But they were somewhat tainted with bittersweet hues. My homeland had become alien to me. Idi Amin had ultimately decided that this was no longer my home.

CHAPTER TWELVE
1963 - Kakira, Uganda
Age 10

"I'm hungry, Miah," Kimo said, kicking a can onto the street.

"You're always hungry," I gibed.

He reached into the pockets of his little khaki shorts and pulled out the lining on both sides, stretching the stitching to its limits.

"See, I've got nothing," he whined.

"Go back home and get something to eat then," I said, giggling at his self-pity.

"Are you crazy? I'll get some lovely food from my Maa, but in return she'll make me sit and do hours of homework. I can't afford to pay that price," he said, shaking his head.

Reaching into my pocket, I took out the ten-cent coin I'd been saving.

"Look what I have," I bragged. Kimo's eyes glistened with glee.

"We can get two portions of fried mogo chips with this," I said, waving the coin at him.

"Yes please! I like my mogo chips to be absolutely drenched in chilli and lemon," Kimo said, licking his lips. "My Aunty Vanita calls it 'cassava root' in her posh accent when her friends come for chai," he chuckled.

We made our way to the Halwai shop not far from us. Along the way I dreamt of all the mouth-watering confectioneries that would be on display. Saffron tinted deep-fried jalebi swirls, topped with sticky syrup. The mint green pistachio sweets with soft fudge-like textures were my favourite. All of the delicious Indian treats were divine, but this kind of luxury came at a price. With just ten cents, we could only afford simple fried mogo chips.

Upon entering the Halwai shop, we were greeted by a bouquet of aromas and colours. A little bell rang above the door, alerting the proprietor. Anand-Lal Mukherji hobbled out from behind his counter. He was a short, stocky old man with a neatly kept, well-oiled mustache, sporting specks of grey. Anand-Lal's teeth stood out the most; deep crimson from chewing tobacco, which he stored in his cheeks like a hamster. He waited for a few moments, chomping away as he scanned our appearance.

"Yes… how can I help?" he said plainly, not expecting much of a sale from ten-year-olds. I winked at Kimo.

"Uncle, what have you got in store today?" I asked.

Menus or lists of stock were seldom displayed, as every day there would be a contrast of tasty offerings for sale depending on what his wife freshly cooked up in the kitchen quarters. Anand-Lal would verbally reel off a list of sweets and snacks. It would take him a good forty to fifty seconds, to make his way through the list.

"—and that's everything we have today. What would you boys like then?" he said.

Kimo and I gave each other a little nudge before I replied.

"Uncle, can I just have two portions of mogo chips

please? I only have ten cents," I said, grinning like a chimpanzee, holding up my measly coin.

"What? So why did you ask for the entire list of items? Honestly. This new generation! No common sense. Wasting my time!" he grumbled, whilst packing the mogo into paper bags.

"Here. Now off you go!" he muttered, taking my puny offering and sending us on our way.

"You're so cheeky, Miah," Kimo giggled, tucking into his portion.

"Let's come back tomorrow after school. I have another plan," I said, with a flicker of mischief.

That evening I waited for Adha to come home from work. Upon entering the house, Adha would always hang his jacket on the hook behind the door, throw his garage keys on the kitchen worktop after greeting Maa, and then make his way to the bathroom.

Like clockwork, he walked through the door.

As soon as he'd entered the bathroom, I made a grab for his jacket and reached into his inside pocket.

"Yes!" I whispered, clasping his cigarette box. After tearing off much of the inner foil and slipping it into my pocket, I ensured everything was back in its place. The next morning, I pleaded with Maa to donate ten cents to me. She was fed up of me scrounging for more pocket money than I deserved. I would tell her she was the best Maa in the world. She would slap her palm firmly across her forehead, knowing that I'd hound her 'til I got my way. After school the next day, Kimo and I jumped off our bus by the oil mill.

"Miah, I had the most boring Maths class today with Mr Thakar. He made us die a thousand deaths with his droning voice. Algebra is a torture weapon," Kimo complained, dragging his feet, pulling his sliding rucksack onto his frail shoulders.

"Don't worry. Your day is about to get brighter," I chuckled.

Kimo saw the Halwai shop come into sight.

"Are you treating me again, Miah? What's this plan you have?" he said.

"Let me lead," I said, giving him the infamous wink.

The bell rang and Anand-Lal Mukherji came out from behind his tall counter. He was so well hidden behind it, that he'd often startle customers if they weren't aware of his presence.

"You two again! More mogo, I assume?" he said, scanning us from head to toe once more.

"Uncle, what do you have in store today?" I asked cunningly.

"I'm not wasting time again, reciting the entire list, when all you have is ten cents. Now, do you want mogo or not?" he grunted, with a scowl on his face.

I pulled out what looked like a larger coin from my pocket and tossed it in the air, catching it in the palm of my hands. His expression changed in a matter of seconds.

"Oh, you have a shilling today!" Anand-Lal cheered. "Ok, so today we have, jilebi, gulab jamun, barfi, laddoo, chewra, gathia—" he continued reeling off an almighty list of mouth-watering sweets and savouries.

"So, what will you have, boys?" he asked, with a gluttonous grin, warming his palms.

My teeth were on full display like a Cheshire cat. Opening my fist, I unwrapped the ten-cent coin from the foil and handed it to Anand-Lal.

"Can I have two portions of mogo chips please," I said,

smirking.

Kimo was on the floor curled up tight, clutching his stomach. The occasional squeak of laughter escaped him, some so high pitched, only dogs could hear him.

"What am I going to do with you numbskulls?" Anand-Lal yelled, holding his head. "Here, take your mogo and go!"

We left the shop, eyes streaming with tears, as per usual.

"You were right, Miah—you really brightened up my day" Kimo chuckled.

CHAPTER THIRTEEN
16th October 1972 - Kakira, Uganda
Age 19

"I'll manage, Tito. It won't take me long, don't worry. You carry on helping the neighbours with Uncle Usman," I said, grabbing the woven shopping bag that Maa used for the markets.

"Don't buy too much, or it'll go to waste. Just get some basic fruits and veg for now, brother," Tito said, putting his shoes on before he headed next door with my uncle.

Boarding the bus to the markets, I pondered over how much had changed. Buses were normally packed with locals, but there seemed to be fewer and fewer of them going about their daily activities. Perhaps that was because many had already left Uganda. The atmosphere was eerie; the bus was barren. Maa and I would often catch the bus to the markets when I was younger. I'd carry her shopping and receive ten cents in return. The thought of mogo chips momentarily swept over me. There would be happy faces chattering away, discussing recipes, weddings, parties, and festivals. Little children would be playing games on their seats, chatting away to one another.

The vibe on that particular day, however, was sombre, dull, and intimidating.

The bus reached my stop, and I disembarked. No smile from the driver.

The market was only another two minutes away on foot. After being deep in thought about what supplies I needed, I'd unexpectedly found myself near an open top army vehicle with three of Amin's soldiers sitting inside. They were parked outside the barbershop, laughing, in conversation. One of them appeared to have a bottle of beer in his hands.

"Muhindi. Oy! Muhindi!" blared one of the soldiers.

Fear struck every vein in my body as I looked back.

"Why is your hair so long, Muhindi? Come here, to this barbershop and get it cut! Or if you want, I will cut it for you," he cackled. The other soldiers found it hilarious. My aim was to get to the market as quickly as possible. I increased my pace, trying not to make it obvious to the soldiers that I was petrified.

I crossed the road and managed to disappear into a small crowd that had gathered behind a mango truck. I kept glancing back to see if any of them had followed me, but they weren't to be seen. Upon entering the market area, I gained some comfort and solace. There were plenty of people around me, so I didn't feel as threatened. But I needed to make my way out of there soon.

Twenty minutes later, I cautiously made my way out of the market gates. The army vehicle was still there.

"What do I do now?" I whispered to myself.

Glancing at my watch, I realised there would be a bus waiting to leave soon from the bus stand. I walked on, with the bag of fruit and veg tightly clasped in my hands.

The army vehicle slowly appeared in my peripheral vision. I began to pray.

"Oy! Muhindi! Why have you still not cut your hair? I thought I told you earlier to cut it!" shouted one of the soldiers.

Avoiding any eye contact this time, I briskly continued.

"Don't you ignore me, Muhindi!" he shouted, following with more Swahili slurs.

My power walk transformed into a jog. Luckily, I spotted my bus, a hundred yards away at the most.

"Come back you son of a—" the soldier called out, before jumping out of his vehicle, running towards me.

Glancing back, I caught sight of him smashing his beer bottle against a metal pole as he bolted, waving the remaining half in the air. He had a noticeable wide pink scar that stretched from the top of his left eyebrow, all the way down to his chin, a previous knife wound perhaps.

"I'm gonna scalp you today, Muhindi! How dare you ignore me?"

My heart felt like it had stopped beating, but my legs just kept going, as if independent from my body, peddling at a hundred kilometres an hour. My hair swamped in perspiration against my face and neck. He was only nine or ten yards behind me. My bus was about to depart.

"Stop, Muhindi!" he shouted once more.

The ticket conductor began to close the door, as it moved away. With inches to spare, I managed to slip in; my shopping bag wasn't so fortunate. The outraged soldier was left behind, stomping on every last bit of food I'd purchased. Even though I was safe now, I'd never felt so frightened in all my years living in Uganda. My heart didn't stop thumping till I'd gotten off at my stop. I ran towards my home as fast as I could. In my mind's eye the air had turned black, the trees had lost their colours and the path had turned to ashes.

"What happened to you?" Tito yelled, running to me from the neighbour's front porch.

"Amin's soldiers. One of them chased me onto the bus with a glass bottle when I left the market. I made it in time, but without the shopping bag. I lost it," I said, gazing down at the ground, tears streaming.

"Ok come inside, Amiri, you need to freshen up. I'll make you a nice cup of chai. Don't worry about the shopping," Tito said, taking me by the arm and guiding me inside. He sat me down on the settee and headed off to the kitchen. Almost immediately, my fear turned into anger. All I could think about was how my life had been devalued since Amin declared the expulsion order. From being born in the Pearl of Africa, belonging to its soil, spending my sweet childhood here, dreaming of my future in this magnificent country, this was suddenly what my life had become. After nineteen years of living on this land, I was now a stranger. A foreigner with no rights, an unwanted body. If I hadn't made it to the bus on time, I would have become an unwanted corpse.

"Amir! Are you ok?" Uncle Usman called as he rushed in.

"I'm ok, I just had a close shave with a soldier today—almost," I said, running my fingers through my hair.

"What? What did he do? Where was he?"

"He chased me onto the bus from the market. I dropped the shopping," I muttered.

"These rascals have no respect for anyone! Just because the deadline is looming, it doesn't mean we deserve to be treated like dirt!" he shouted. I had rarely witnessed my uncle so angry. "The quicker we leave, the better. I've arranged for you to go in Miko's van to Kampala tomorrow for your passport. He's taking a few more people from our village, so you won't be alone. Get your paperwork together in your satchel. I'll give you some money to take with you. You'll be leaving very early to avoid queuing too long. So, get an early night tonight and try not to worry too much", he said, putting his hand firmly on my shoulder. It was clearly him who was worried to death.

"Are we going to make it out from here?" I asked him, gazing into his eyes.

"We will soon. We will."

CHAPTER FOURTEEN
1958 - Iganga, Uganda
Age 5

Our house in Iganga was small and simple, but it had picturesque views of the vast Ugandan landscape. We had a quaint little garden at the front, lined with flower beds and a mini white picket fence. However, my brothers and I knocked part of it down with our football. Maa was just pleased it wasn't the flowers. My older brother Aziz was behind the damaging blow. He would get too competitive. Maa blew steam like a pressure cooker if she caught us kicking a ball around her precious flowerbeds. At the back we had various fruits and vegetables growing. I still remember holding Maa's hand when we would pick ripe mangoes from the tree. Aziz would climb up and toss them down, consistently aiming for my head. Ugandan soil is well known for its fertile qualities. You could effortlessly toss a few seeds onto the ground and you're almost guaranteed growth within a matter of days.

I distinctly remember my sister, Nidah's birth. There was so much excitement in the air, with neighbours and friends fussing around Maa. Many women would come to the door with food, treats and knitted baby garments. Many of them would kneel to my level and patronise me.
"Do you know you're going to be a big brother soon?

Would you like a baby brother or sister?" they would ask. I would normally respond with a squint. What I wanted was to go straight into the kitchen and tuck into the sweets that had arrived.

It wasn't long before Maa had the baby. Or babies, I should say. We were all surprised by that fact that she'd had twins, including the village Doula, who was perplexed at having examined such a minor baby bump for months. We were all so delighted that the day had finally arrived.

My Aunty Mumtaz, Maa's younger sister who lived with us in Iganga, was doing her best to restrain me outside in the garden.

"Wait, just a little longer, Amir. You can't go in right now. Wait until we are told we can go inside, for goodness' sake," she pleaded, pulling me back by both of my arms.

"But I want to go see Maa. Let me go! I've been waiting here forever. Let me go see the babies!" I yelled, freeing one of my arms from her grip.

The Doula emerged from the front door. As she walked past us, I cried out to her. "I want to see Maa! Why can't I go in?"

"Sweetheart, just give your Maa some time. She needs to rest," she calmly responded.

The Doula glanced at Aunty Mumtaz. Her eyes had a look of defeat and I sensed something unspoken pass between her and my Aunt. Wisps of her silver hair had escaped her multicoloured head wrap and droplets of perspiration covered her neck and upper lip. Her beaded sandalwood necklace glistened in the sun.

Disturbed by the silence, I freed my other arm, slipping out of Aunty Mumtaz's grasp. Upon entering the front door, I made my way along the hallway wondering why I couldn't hear the sound of a baby crying. In the doorway to Maa's bedroom, I witnessed Adha holding something wrapped in a yellow crochet blanket. Suddenly a little foot popped out and curled up.

"Adha, is that one of our babies? Aunty Mumtaz told me we have two. Are they girls or boys?" I asked inquisitively, scrambling onto a stool next to Adha to get a better view.

"This is your new baby sister, Nidah", Adha whispered, gently tilting her towards me.

She was such an angelic vision; she mesmerised me.

"Hello, Nidah. I'm Amir, your big brother. I'll let you play with all my toys. I'll look after you too. I promise," I said, stroking her blanket wrapped around her tiny doll-like frame.

"Adha, where's the other baby? Is it a girl or a boy?" I beamed, excited to meet my other sibling.

My father's smile dissolved, and his eyes filled with sorrow.

I looked to Maa for answers. She was laid in her bed, also with a little bundle wrapped in a cream blanket.

"Maa! I missed you today," I cried, jumping down off the stool, running towards her. Trying desperately to catch sight of the baby, I gently leaned over. Maa didn't look at me the whole time. She was still and silent, gazing at the beautiful little being in her arms.

"Maa?" I said, feeling unsettled. I couldn't understand why she wouldn't respond to me. "Maa, is this my baby brother or sister? What name have you kept?" I said, still attempting to coax an answer from her.

"This was your baby brother," she muttered. A tear fell from her eyes and disappeared into the blanket.

"Why isn't he moving Maa? Is he sleeping?" I asked, stroking his little nose.

"He's fallen asleep forever. He won't wake up now. We have to say goodbye and send him to Allah's house. He'll sleep there peacefully," she said. Her voice was calm, but the pain on her face sent tremors through me. More of her tears descended.

I wondered where Allah's house was, and why Maa would send my new baby brother away.

"Maa he can sleep in my room. Please don't send him away. I promise I won't make any noise. I'll look after him," I pleaded.

"I know, my sweetheart. But he must go," she replied, her voice trembling.

CHAPTER FIFTEEN

1960 - Iganga, Uganda
Age 7

"Come on, Nidah, find it. Where is it?" I said, encouraging my toddling sister to keep looking.

"Kokolate," she mumbled, lifting the cushions from our settee.

"Keep looking. Where's Mr Teddy? Maybe he's hiding the chocolate?" I teased, pointing to her favourite plush toy.

She ran over and lifted Mr Teddy into the air.

"Kokolate!" she yelled with glee. "Naughty Teddy," she said, briefly scolding her little friend, before giving him a friendly hug.

She tucked into her treat within seconds. She would have gobbled it whole, had I not stepped in to remove the foil wrapper.

"Amir, you know what Nidah is like. Now she's had chocolate, she won't touch her dinner. She barely eats enough as it is. You're seven years old now, you're a big boy. You should understand," Aunty Mumtaz explained, with her hands resting on her hips.

Aunty Mumtaz was more of an older sister to us than an aunt. She would often join in our forbidden ball games in the garden and enjoyed card games with us. She would also share domestic duties with Maa and Johari. Cooking, cleaning, washing, helping us get ready for school and also helping out during mealtimes. Aunty Mumtaz was only ten years older than me. Her mother died whilst giving birth to her, hence why Maa took on many responsibilities from a young age and raised her.

On our way to a local wedding one day, I remember skipping down the street with Maa holding Nidah in her arms and Aunty Mumtaz leading the way towards the very last house. The property was fully built from corrugated iron. Handmade wildflower garlands were draped over the doorway and many women and children were gathered outside singing songs in their finest outfits. They were congregated around in a circle, sitting on large woven picnic blankets and colourful cushions, decorated with sequins. The lady in the centre was playing a double-sided drum, known as a dholki, whilst people sang along to the beat. It wasn't long before food was being served. Queueing in the heat was the worst part. Giant steel pots, twice as high as me, were placed outside and guests were filling up their plates with lamb pilau, chicken tikka, kebabs and samosas. We found a little spot on the blankets and sat down to eat, our plates overflowing.

From a young age, I was never a big eater and whatever I did eat was never chewed properly, unless it was a sweet dish. After inhaling my food, I wanted to catch a glimpse of the bride and groom and also take a look around the house. As I got up to go, my sister began to follow me.

"Nidah, sweetie, you stay here with me. You need to finish your meal", Maa said, waving for her to come back. Holding Nidah's hand, I led her back to Maa and sat her down next to my Aunty Mumtaz, who was struggling to feed her. Nidah wasn't showing any sign of compliance. Aunty Mumtaz turned to Maa,

"Jilu, she's not eating at all. What shall I do? She refused breakfast this morning too," she said, as she placed her head in her hands. Her distress was obvious.

"She was a little feverish last night. Perhaps she's still not feeling too well," Maa said, pressing her palm against Nidah's forehead. "I'll take her home. You stay here with Amir and finish your meal. Come home whenever you're ready", Maa said, gathering up the pleats of her peach silk sari.

Maa was known to be one of the most fashionable ladies in the village. Most of the time she would wear long frocks in the latest cotton prints, which she made herself, on her Singer sewing machine, using fabric sourced at nearby markets. She would also make dresses and carry out alterations for others in the village, which proved to be an ample second income for our household. Maa also loved Saris, but only really wore them at weddings or festivals. She only had a few but looked after them well.

"I want to go inside and see the bride and groom. I'll be back," I shouted to my aunt. Before she could respond, I slipped through the crowds gathered by the door. Managing to squeeze through the gaps in the bodies, I made my way into what seemed like the living room area. It was difficult to tell. People were packed like tilapia in crates at the fish market. A concoction of odours such as perfume, aftershave, flowers, chicken curry and sweat, hung in the air. It was difficult to breathe. There was a small, two-seater mahogany bench, with a padded topper covered in emerald green fabric. On the bench was the bride, embellished from head to toe in a blood red sari with gold sequins. Her face was hidden underneath a red veil with a golden foil fringe. Her henna adorned hands were visible, neatly placed on her lap, one on top of the other with a little gold band twinkling away on her ring finger. The groom was sporting a smart brown blazer, a crisp white shirt and a brown tie, with matching brown bell bottoms. A long flower garland made of alternate yellow and white carnations hung around his neck. On a little table in the corner of the room, behind the bride, was a picture of Krishna, a Hindu God. At either side of the frame, two incense sticks were alight, embedded into coconuts. In front of the frame was a small box of jalebis and laddoos.

"Bingo," I whispered. Sweets were always stashed near the happy couple at every wedding.

Many people were coming in to meet and congratulate the newly-weds. My opportunity came when a large family with three very tall boys entered to greet them. They were tall enough to block everyone's view of me filling up my little pockets with laddoos. I gave the jalebis a miss. They were too sticky to conceal.

One of the tall boys looked over his shoulders and spotted me. He gave me a little smile and whispered, "Those are an offering to God."

"I know. He asked me to come and get them for him," I whispered back, trying to act as convincing as possible.

He instantly burst into laughter.

Eventually, I managed to sneak out of the house, only to find Aunty Mumtaz standing outside, frowning.

"I've been looking for you! Where were you?" she yelled.

"I was in the house. I wanted to see the bride and groom," I chimed with a cheeky smile.

"What's in your pockets? What did you take?" She asked, spotting the suspicious bulges on either side of my shorts.

Grinning from ear to ear, I whispered, "laddoos."
"Here take one," I said.

My aunt never refused sweets.

It was getting late, so we decided to head back home.

"Why do wedding laddoos always taste the best Aunty?" I asked, savouring the delights of my third helping.

"Because they're free," she giggled.

"Does God like to share things with us, Aunty?" I asked.

"God? Yes! Of course he does. God is kind," she said with a smile.

As we approached the house, we saw Doctor Anwar departing, with Adha waving to him from the front door. Doctor Anwar was the local medic and herbalist. He was the first point of call if there were any accidents or illnesses within the village.

Aunty Mumtaz and I sped over to my father.

"What's happened, Adha? Is it Maa? Is she ok?" I asked.

Adha hesitated for a moment. He pursed his lips together and took a deep breath.

"It's Nidah. She's not very well. Her fever has come back, and it's very high."

A deadly silence followed. "Don't worry though. We just have to monitor her. She'll be fine. Yes. Just fine," Adha said, sounding as though he was trying to reassure himself.

I made my way into my parents' room. Nidah was laid in their bed, as silent as can be. She was wide awake with her gaze firmly fixed on the ceiling. I was bewildered to see her like this. She would never sit still, unless chocolate was on offer.

"Nidah, sweetheart. Try to get some rest. Close your eyes, my baby," Maa said, soothing her as much as she could. Maa was always very protective of her little girl. Even a slight bump or scratch on Nidah would send Maa into a panic. But we knew all too well that Maa feared losing Nidah. She'd already lost her little boy two years prior.

Forty-eight hours had passed. Maa spent every one of those hours glued to the side of the bed, closely monitoring Nidah. Everyone in the household was anxious yet hopeful. But Nidah wasn't showing any signs of recovery. Her fever continued to soar, and Doctor Anwar was once again summoned to our home. Aziz, Aunty Mumtaz and I were watching from outside my parents' room as the door was left ajar. We were told to wait in the hallway but crept closer to see what was happening.

"Be quiet you two," Aunty Mumtaz whispered, trying to hush Aziz and I, who were pulling each other back from the small door frame, desperate to catch a glimpse.

"I'm afraid it's Pneumonia," Doctor Anwar said, pulling out some pills from his medical bag.

"I had an inkling when you first called me. I've brought a supply of medicine from the hospital which you need to give to her three times a day," he said. I saw him pass Maa a small brown jar of tablets.

"Can't we just take her to the hospital now?" Maa

asked. I could hear the despair in her voice.

"You could, but the doctors there will give you the same medicine and tell you that—" Doctor Anwar paused and took a deep breath.

"And tell me what?" Maa yelled, demanding an answer.

"That she —she has a fifty-fifty chance of survival. If Nidah doesn't respond to these medicines, I'm afraid there's not much else that can be done, even in hospital. Keep her comfortable and stay on top of her pills," he said. I saw him close his bag and roll down his shirt sleeves.

"No! This can't be right! What are you saying? This information is wrong," Maa exclaimed. She stood up, breathing into the palms of her hands deeply.

"Jilu, calm yourself. If you start panicking now, it's not going to help anyone. Just listen to the instructions given. Pray for her. Everything will be ok by the grace and mercy of Allah," Adha said. He sounded frantic as he tried to reassure Maa.

"I'll be back tomorrow evening to administer more fluids. Until then, stay by her side and carry on with the medication. Please come and get me if you have any concerns or if she gets any worse. I'll come straight away no matter what time of day it is," Doctor Anwar said, as he got up to leave. Aunty Mumtaz, Aziz and I, bolted away from the door to the other end of the hallway.

Our world had turned upside down. These were my first experiences of fear, dread and anxiety. It was the very first time I'd felt my stomach churn. The sight of my mother crying her eyes out, and my father heartbroken, was something I'd witnessed two years earlier when we lost my baby brother. This time it frightened me to my very core, as I understood so much more. I hesitantly approached Maa.

"Maa, don't worry. Doctor Anwar has given medicine to Nidah. She will get better now. I promise. Please don't cry," I muttered, wiping her tears away with my palms.

Aunty Mumtaz suddenly let out a huge shriek. She grabbed a towel that was hanging on the back of the door and ran towards the window above Maa's bed, waving it frantically in the air.

"Shoo! Shoo. Get away!" she yelled.

We were all startled by her actions and Maa was about to shout at her for creating a scene, before we'd realised what it was.

"Was that—"

"An owl, yes, Jilu. Sorry for giving you all a fright. But they're bad luck," she said, clutching the towel in her hands.

Aunty Mumtaz, along with Maa, and plenty of other Indian ladies in the village, were extremely superstitious. Especially with owls and black cats. They apparently carried evil omens. Many would light incense sticks or chant mantras before going about their daily activities. However, Maa would always get out her prayer mat and say an extra prayer.

Maa stayed by Nidah's side all night. She kept wetting flannels and applying them to her forehead, soothing her as she slept.

I spent most of the following day playing with the neighbour's young boy, Lalit, who was two years my senior, and his cute little dog, Oscar. The dog was an unusual mixed breed. Possibly a sheep dog mixed with a german shepherd. Oscar would make a special effort whenever I was around, wagging his tail, ready for a game of fetch. The sun was setting, and the sky had turned a deep shade of orange. We were in Lalit's back garden enjoying Oscar's company.

"Lalit, throw me the stick, it's my turn now," I pleaded, dying to throw it for Oscar to catch. He would jump incredibly high, soaring through the air.

"Ok here, catch!" he yelled, throwing the stick my way.

"Amir!" came a loud call out of nowhere.

Thud! The stick clonked me on the back of my head as my attention wandered.

"Lalit! Careful," I shouted.

"Amir!" the voice came again. It was Aunty Mumtaz.

"Coming!" I shouted, praying everything was ok.

My back garden was accessible from Lalit's, via a small gate through the wooden fence that bordered the two properties. Arriving at the back door where Aunty Mumtaz was waiting for me, I could see that her eyes were red and puffy, and her cheeks damp.

"What's wrong?" I asked, apprehensive about what was going on.

"Amir, Nidah—she's—Nidah has—" Aunty Mumtaz couldn't finish her sentence.

Trying to make sense, I tuned in to the background noise. It was the sound of Maa wailing in pain.

My legs turned to jelly as I made my way to Maa's bedroom, like a foal taking its first steps.

Nidah was laying there, lifeless, in my mother's arms. Doctor Anwar had his arm around Adha, whose face was concealed in his handkerchief. Aziz was silent in the corner of the room, his eyes swollen. Gently, I approached

Maa.

"Maa? What's happened to Nidah?" I asked, my eyes filling up from the sadness that had engulfed the room.

"She's gone, sweetheart. She's gone to be with your little brother in Allah's house," she whispered to me, whilst her tears carried on rolling, her lips so dry they'd cracked.

At age seven, I'd just about understood that death meant having to go to Allah's house. What I couldn't quite fathom, was why you couldn't come back from there and whether his house was close by.

Some weeks after Nidah's funeral, I asked Maa, "Why can't Nidah come back? I miss her."

"She's in Allah's house now, Amir. Once you go to God's house, you can't return. Don't worry though, Allah takes care of everyone who goes to him," she calmly explained.

"No! That's not right. She needs to come home because this is her house. I'm going to Allah's house right now to bring her back. It's the house across from the bicycle shop, isn't it? The one with the bright blue door? I'm going right now, Maa," I yelled, stamping my feet in fury.

Maa grabbed hold of me and embraced me tightly—before she cried again.

CHAPTER SIXTEEN

17th October 1972 - Kakira, Uganda
Age 19

Miko was a devout follower of Milton Obote. Since Amin's military dictatorship had overthrown Obote's stance in Uganda, Miko had kept a considerably low profile. He didn't share his opinions as publicly as he did before and kept his political views covert.

He worked as a supervisor in a bank and was well-known for his random acts of kindness. We adored him for his helpful and charitable nature. A faithful follower of Christianity and an ambassador for community cohesion, he successfully integrated with many Indian families, and we often spotted him at Indian weddings and festivals, showing off his language skills in Gujarati.

My family and I were first acquainted with Miko when his pet goose migrated to our backyard to lay eggs. After that first time, it became a regular occurrence. Nevertheless, once she'd laid them, they would miraculously disappear. Coincidentally, Maa would rustle up the tastiest omelettes we'd ever eaten on those particular days. Miko would eventually turn up at our door, asking if we'd seen his goose. We became good friends thereafter. He never learned of the eggs.

A vehicle beeped its horn from outside the house.
"Amir, go! He's here. Have you got your documents?"

Uncle Usman called.

"Yup, I've got them," I replied, closing the zip on my satchel, feeling confident.

My uncle wandered towards me. "Keep in mind what I told you about money and keeping your wallet hidden. The passport offices are filled with loyal workers who won't charge more than the set rate for processing. But still, take the extra cash I gave you and keep it well out of sight," he reminded me.

Outside, Miko was waiting in his eight-seater van, which had seen better days. It legally only had space for seven people. The back two seats had a gap in between, in which Miko had stuffed a makeshift wobbly wooden stool with a folded blanket on top. We'd often tell him in the garage, it wasn't safe to do so. But he was totally disinterested in our safety advice. He called it his eight-seater dream machine, despite it being on its last legs.

The vehicle appeared to be full of passengers.

"Come, Amiri. I have a seat for you right at the back," he said, waving his arm outside the window.

As I made my way over, I noticed several rust spots near his wheels. I figured there was no point in offering him a deal at the garage to fix those.

Some passengers disembarked, politely offering me room to squeeze into the back, while I desperately prayed not to get lumbered with the wooden stool. Thankfully, I didn't.

There was an Indian family who I didn't recognise. Two young boys aged around ten & eleven, their mother, father and their grandmother. An older gentleman occupied the passenger seat up front next to Miko. He looked to be in his late sixties, well dressed with a very expensive looking watch on show. I remember thinking how foolish he was to parade his possessions like that, especially in the climate we were faced with.

Being one of the younger ones, it was inevitable that I ended up at the back, but luckily, I was in a comfortable seat. The two boys were sitting next to me; the youngest having drawn the short straw after his mother had demanded that he move onto the wooden stool to make room for me.

Both of the boys were wearing matching bucket hats and playing with a deck of cards, and the rest of the passengers were busy engaged in conversation. We'd finally set off from Kakira to Kampala. The mother and grandmother of the two boys opened some large tiffins filled with vegetable samosas and onion bhajis, still hot and fresh. I'll never forget their kindness as they shared their snacks amongst us. Tucking into the samosas reminded me of Maa. For a moment, I closed my eyes and imagined I was sitting in Adha's car with the rest of my family, heading out for a picnic. Maa would always end up giving us a samosa each on the journey, just to keep us quiet.

After a quick stop in Jinja to stretch our legs and freshen up, we headed back on the road again. I'd had my fill of the window view and fresh air, so I entertained the boys with some card tricks. They gazed wide-eyed at some of the illusions I had up my sleeve.

"Can you teach me how to do that, please! That was the best trick in the world," the older child jabbered, mesmerised.

"Of course I will. We also have the journey back. I can teach you plenty of tricks," I responded with a smile. Kimo briefly flashed through my mind.

"Miko, where are we? Shouldn't we be there by now,"

asked the older gentleman at the front.

"I'm not sure, you know. I might have taken a wrong turn. Maybe I should turn back," Miko said, scratching his head.

"This is Mabira Forest, Miko. We need to get back to the main road," the father of the boys stated, looking agitated and restless.

"Papa look!" cried one of the boys, pointing outside the window.

Everyone shuffled to take a look.

"Oh, my Lord! Ok, we need to move fast," Miko gasped.

My heart began to race. I still couldn't see what was outside and Miko's reaction was unsettling. He spun the vehicle around and headed back, giving me a clearer view of what was causing such a stir.

Three bloodied bodies were scattered on the ground. They seemed to be young African men. One of them lay there with an amputated arm situated a few metres away from the body. I couldn't believe what I'd witnessed.

The passengers were distraught. Funnily enough, the children didn't seem to be as frightened as what I'd expected. They continued to gape at the scene with their jaws hanging, 'til it was no longer in plain sight. The atmosphere in the van mirrored that of the murky clouds outside; dark and eerie. My stomach felt irritated by every bump in the road. We approached some enormous iron gates and hoped there would be someone nearby to guide us or give direction. Miko stuck his head out of the window and yelled to get some attention.

The gates opened abruptly. Miko drove the van forward, looking left and right as he did so.

A surge of angry men dived out from behind the trees and surrounded the vehicle; their guns dispensing bullet after bullet as they fired into the air.

The passengers began to scream. We heard Miko shouting "No, no, we are lost, we are lost. We need help. Please."

Realising that they weren't a rebel group from their uniforms gave us temporary relief. But terror took over when we recognised them. Amin's soldiers.

"That's the soldier who tried to scalp me yesterday outside the market! That's him! He'll kill me if he recognises me," I cried out with shock.

The distinct scar on his face was one I'd never forget. My body had frozen over and I felt as if I was falling into a dark abyss.

The father of boys turned around, "Don't panic, take my son's hat and wear it over your head. Tuck your hair under. He'll remember you if you stand out," he said, swiping his son's hat and handing it to me. "Stay calm everyone, try not to panic," he whispered, holding his wife's hand.

Pulling the hat over my head, I did my best to tuck every lock of hair under it.

"Turn off the engine and step outside. NOW!" the soldier roared.

Miko immediately conformed and stepped outside. The soldier rammed the butt of his gun into Miko's shoulders and he staggered to his knees. The passengers began to shriek.

With the barrel of his gun tightly pressed against Miko's neck, he snarled at another soldier, ordering him to empty the vehicle. They herded everyone out like cattle.

"Come on, quickly, quickly," he yelled.

As I stepped out, I briefly looked up and could see part of the soldier's face. That was him—the same terrifying scar. Tilting my head down, with most of my face concealed, I followed the rest of the passengers who were being led over to a shaded area under some trees.

I wondered whether I would be killed today, or worse—tortured.

Was this my time? Would my family ever know what happened to me? Would my body be left decomposing in the jungle, like the ones we saw earlier? Or would they gather up our carcasses and feed the crocodiles in Lake Victoria?

Forced to kneel under a tree in formation, the scarred soldier paced up and down along the line, assessing us carefully, while we gazed at the soil beneath us, trembling with uncertainty. The soldier's boots stopped suddenly in front of me and my heart stopped with them. Time was unfathomable in those moments. Buried in despair, I envisioned my family, my mother's smile, my father arriving home from work and my siblings playing. Nidah's giggles surged through my mind, like an electric current, striking. He was on the move again and this time he approached Miko, who was still on the gravel path on his knees, breathing heavily, with a gun pressed firmly against his neck.

"Why are you here? Tell me."

"I'm sorry, Sir, I took a wrong turn and I got lost. Please, we mean no harm," Miko responded.

The soldier cackled as Miko knelt helplessly on the ground, in tears. I felt sick in my stomach. These men were vile and had no respect for anyone's life.

"Leave him alone," shouted the older gentleman.

Suddenly the soldier's attention turned to us. He paced his way back to our line, displaying an arrogant strut.

"You want to be a big hero, Muhindi?" he said to the gentleman in a sinister tone, before brutally slapping his face.

"Oh! I see you have a beautiful watch. How much Ugandan currency did you gather in your greedy pockets to buy this? Tell me, Muhindi?" he fumed.

The grandmother had begun whispering prayers and mantras to herself, rocking back and forth. I also prayed for a divine intervention to save us.

The soldier put down his gun and snatched the watch. Placing it on his own wrist, he waved it in the air to show his fellow soldiers the prize he'd acquired. Another soldier approached and forced us to empty the contents of our bags on the floor. Everyone complied. They took our money, gold earrings from the ladies, along with their wedding bands and bracelets.

The mother gazed into her husband's eyes as she removed her band to surrender. He gave her a nod. She cried without making a sound.

After more than an hour of torment, they decided to let us go. Although we were in the shade, we were drained, dejected and dehumanised. We cautiously lifted our tired bodies and gathered whatever of our belongings the soldiers had tossed aside. Thankfully, my documents were still there, intact. I swiftly gathered them and secured them back in my satchel.

For the whole time we were there, poor Miko was made to kneel with his hands at either side of him, in the scorching heat of the unforgiving midday sun.

They eventually gave him permission to stand and demanded that we get out, or face being shot. We piled into the van as quickly as possible.

As I approached the door, the scarred soldier blocked my passage with his rifle.

"Wait," he said sharply. There was a long pause. An eternity.

"I like your hat, boy. Give this to me," he said.

Just when I thought we were safe, the world collapsed around me. I refused to make eye contact. I couldn't do it.

"Did you not hear what I said, boy?"

My chest was ready to implode. *Was this the end?*

"He can't hear you," came a little voice. It was one of the young boys. "That's my big brother. He was born deaf and dumb. Here, you can take my hat, they're both the same," he said, handing it over. The soldier inspected it for a moment before nodding for us to leave. We climbed into the van, and Miko hurriedly tried to start up the engine—but it wouldn't start.

"Miko hurry up, do something," shouted the mother.

Turning the key again, Miko whispered, "Lord, help us, please."

One of the soldiers began to fire his gun in the air as a sign of impatience. The poor grandmother began praying her mantras even louder, as if trying to control her emotions. The boys were shouting for Miko to hurry.

Miko tried again—the engine finally roared.

"Thank you, God!" Miko yelled. The sweet sound of the motor was music to our ears. My shoulders dropped as I let out a huge sigh of relief.

We departed hastily; tyres screeching. We managed to ultimately find our way back to the main road.

"Everyone, I am driving back to Kakira. It will be too late to join the queue at the office today. If we carry on, the journey will be wasted. We can try again in the coming days," sighed Miko. We were all in agreement and far too traumatised to continue.

CHAPTER SEVENTEEN

1964 - Kakira, Uganda
Age 11

"Line up children. I want an orderly queue," Mrs Patel shouted.

"Why does she always have to yell in our faces?" Kimo whispered, leaning against the school bus.

"So that the children at the back of the line can hear me, Kimo," Mrs Patel bellowed, aiming her gaze at him. "Now stand up straight!" she barked.

Kimo became flustered, his cheeks were beetroot.

She continued on. "Now listen carefully. If during this school trip, I find out that any one of you has misbehaved or not adhered to my instructions, I will march you all back on to this bus and we will head straight back to school, where appropriate punishment will be carried out. Do you understand me?" she roared, leaving Kimo and I almost deaf.

"Yes, Mrs Patel," the class replied in a communal drone.

"And you two! If you do anything to ruin this trip, you watch what happens," she hissed.

Her rage was off the charts with us both. I didn't blame her though. We were a nightmare to handle.

A voice muttered from behind us, "Yeah, Amir. You'll get the cane again if you misbehave."

I knew this brave little wretch very well.

"Shut up, Sarita. You think you're so clever. If you don't be quiet, one of Lake Victoria's crocodiles will be using your fake plait to floss its teeth after eating you," I muttered, with an evil glare. Sarita was a well-known teacher's pet, and always the first to answer questions correctly in class. She won the Student of the Year award every year, without fail. Although she had a few friends, most of the kids struggled to accept her tattletale attitude. She was Mrs Patel's little minion who went squealing to her at every opportune moment.

"My plait is not fake! How dare you?" she said, clutching at her synthetic hair piece.

Sarita, along with many other girls, wore a woven piece of wool in her hair. These pieces were usually wrapped in a plait and then tied with a red silky ribbon at the bottom; generally to help lengthen and thicken it.

"Now follow me children. Make sure you stay in pairs and do not wander off from our group. Is that clear!" Mrs Patel said once more.

The class droned their agreement again. I let out a long sigh, tired from her constant lecturing.

"I'm watching you two."

"Yes, Mrs Patel," I responded sarcastically.

"Yes, Mrs Patel," Sarita mocked.

For once, Kimo and I were keenly processing the information the proprietors gave us, about how the factory operated and about the locally sourced wood they used to make their matches with. The fun part was when we all watched a short bulky row of five hundred matches being lit by the manager. It was his end of tour party trick outside the factory's backyard grassland. They all set alight, like a shooting star, firing across a long metal tray, before he put the flames out with a gallon of water from a plastic barrel. All of the children clapped and cheered.

"We will make our way back to the bus in a moment. Get back into pairs and wait for my instructions," ordered Mrs Patel.

"Miah. Look on the floor," Kimo said, pointing to the ground. "Isn't that the powder used on the tips of the matches?" he asked.

"I think you're right, Kimo, it is."

We could see residue scattered all over the ground in little pockets.

"Shall we light it?" Kimo asked with a devilish grin.

"Are you crazy? The whole place will set on fire!" I cried out, taken aback by Kimo's insane notion.

Luckily no one heard us, and Mrs Patel was at the front, busy flirting with the manager.

"Shh... keep your voice down, Miah. I slipped a few matches in my pocket from inside the factory when no one was looking," he giggled.

Lifting my palm to my forehead, I held it there, shaking my head from left to right.

"Kimo, you're mad."

We assessed the situation further to see how much powder was actually on the ground and whether it would start a fire.

"No, I don't think we should risk it. What if the whole place burns down?" I pleaded.

Kimo's grin widened. There it was again—that look.

"Kimo? What?" I suspiciously queried.

"Look. Right there. There's a little patch of powder near Sarita. Trust me, I say we light it and frighten her.

It'll fizzle out straight away, but the sparks will be enough to scare the little witch," Kimo assured with a glint in his eyes.

"I guess there's no harm in giving her a fright. She's such a pain. Go on, let's go for it," I giggled.

We headed towards the patch where Sarita stood talking to her friends. Kimo lit a match. After flicking it to the ground, we both darted out of sight.

"Aagh!" cried the girls.

The powder began to smoke, and sparks hurtled everywhere. The sound was much louder than we'd expected, like firecrackers at a Diwali celebration.

It fizzled out as promptly as it had started. The manager had gone to grab another barrel of water amidst the chaos. There was no need for it by the time he got back.

He placed the barrel on the ground and gave a stern warning to all of us.

"Who did it?" Mrs Patel screamed out. "If I find out who did, I'll tell you now, you will be expelled from school. Do you understand?"

She was practically breathing fire, as if she'd inhaled the very same powder.

"I saw who did it, Mrs Patel."

A hand shot up from the group. It was Sarita.

"I saw Amir and Kimo light a match. They threw it on the ground and ran away," she said, pointing her index finger directly at us.

"How could you have seen us? You had your back turned to us when we threw it, you blabbermouth," Kimo shouted, before realising what he'd openly declared.

My head was firmly in my palms, with my eyes tightly closed.

"Kimo, Kimo, Kimo—why don't you *think* before you *speak*," I said, reluctantly looking up to see Mrs Patel towering above, ready to slaughter us.

That day we were both suspended from school for a week, along with receiving twelve palm lashes each. It would have been expulsion, had our fathers not pleaded with the school council at an impromptu meeting.

CHAPTER EIGHTEEN
20th October 1972 - Kakira, Uganda
Age 19

Miko's van pulled up outside the house. Approaching the van door, I noticed that the vehicle was empty.

"Amiri! Come sit up front with me," Miko shouted.

Opening the passenger door, I climbed in, with my satchel in tow.

"Where are all the others?" I asked.

"Ah, don't worry about them. They've already left Uganda," he said.

"Really? That was quick! When did they go to Kampala?" I queried.

"They all planned the day after our last trip to collect their paperwork. I was unavailable so I couldn't help them," he said, tapping out a beat on the steering wheel with his fingers.

Personally, I figured they were so disturbed by the previous trip, that they put their foot down to escape as soon as possible. Or perhaps they were too frightened to travel with Miko, in fear of getting lost again.

"Don't worry, Amiri, no wrong turns today. I know exactly where I am going," he said with an optimistic smile, as if he'd read my mind.

Shaking his hand, I reassured him I had confidence in him. At least ninety-five percent.

The journey felt brief, despite the hazy fog of anxiety. There were no pit stops, or any route errors. We reached Kampala early enough for me to join the queue before it grew to an immeasurable size. All my earlier apprehensions receded. Finally, fragments of optimism began to heal some of my angst.

The application process was swift. My passport was finally in my hands with all the paperwork I needed to leave Uganda, once and for all.

Upon walking out of the office, I became overwhelmed and I descended into tears. I stood for at least ten minutes, examining the remaining queue of Ugandan Asians, waiting in anticipation to receive their documents. Their despair was heartbreaking to witness. Only moments before, I'd experienced the same anguish. But there I was, one step closer. Bittersweet emotions swept over me.

"Amiri." A voice came from the street. It was Miko. He looked left and right before darting across the road carrying some mogo chips wrapped in newsprint.

"Are you all done? Did you get your passport?"

"Yes, Miko, thank you! I have it in my satchel," I replied.

"Oh, praise Jesus! Thank goodness you have got it. Amiri, stay positive now. The quicker you leave, the better. Trust me, it will be a fresh start for you and for your family," he said, putting his arm on my shoulder.

"Miko this was once my homeland and now—I'm a foreigner," I cried.

"Amiri, I know. I feel that way too, believe it or not. But you are lucky. You have the choice to leave," Miko said before letting out a tremendous sigh.

Looking up at Miko, I realised that he was suffering just as much at the hands of Amin's soldiers and his dictatorship. Miko's loyalty to Obote was still a tightly kept secret amongst family and friends within our neighbourhood.

We got into his van and hit the road.

"Here, have some mogo. You will miss this when you're in Britain," Miko said with a chuckle.

Unravelling the newspaper brought back so many memories. The smell of freshly fried mogo chips was always one of my most cherished ones. Kimo, the Halwai shop, school days—life. Tucking into my chips, I began thinking about Kimo. I had his address and details, as he'd written quite a few letters to me. *Maybe I'd be able to see him again? What were his living conditions like? Was he safe wherever he was? Was he happy?*

After finishing my chips, I screwed up the newspaper. An image of Idi Amin caught my eye. Promptly flattening it out again on my lap, I read the headline.

'The Future of Asians in Uganda', with a subheading of, *'President Amin will ask the British Government to take responsibility for all Asians in Uganda who are holding British Passports because they are sabotaging the economy of the country.'*

"Don't read that rubbish, Amiri," Miko said.

"Amin is claiming that us *'Muhindis'* are sabotaging Uganda's economy. We are no less than leeches apparently," I grunted.

Miko began shaking his head. "You know, Amiri, it's Idi Amin that needs to go. Don't believe everything you read; you understand me. Asians are holding up the economy, not drowning it," Miko said, gazing ahead into the road.

It was the first time I'd heard Miko make such a bold comment, or any comment for that matter, based on Amin. An hour had passed. Although Miko's radio thundered in the van, the blaring of the tired engine drowned out most of it. The unyielding sun was at its peak, and hunger had set in.

"How long to go Miko?"

"Only one more hour left now, Amiri. We are about to pass Jinja. You want to stop?" Miko asked, reducing his speed.

"Yes, I'm hungry. Can we stop for a bite to eat somewhere?"

Miko raised his eyebrows and nodded.

"There's a mosque nearby, only a few more minutes away. I know the Imam there. His house is attached to the back of the mosque. He's an old friend of mine and it's been a while since I last saw him. If he is still there, maybe we can stop by. Shall we see?" Miko asked. He seemed excited by the idea and I could see that he was hoping I'd agree.

"Sounds like a superb idea. Let's go."

We drove on, before approaching a compact building with iron gates. A small, dilapidated dome was housed on top, covered with what looked like remnants of gold paint. We parked the van outside and opened the gates. The rusty hinges squealed, sending a sharp high-pitched echo that pierced our ears. We glanced around the small yard leading up to the doors of the mosque. Piles of household junk and damaged goods lay scattered on the ground.

Suddenly a man bolted out of the front doors of the mosque, charging towards us, clutching a wooden bat.

"Whoa! Khan Sahib, Khan Sahib, it's me, Miko!" Miko yelled, shielding himself with his arms.

The man looked like he was about to strike Miko, with his bat, until he paused mid-stride, his bat pointing to the clouds.

"Miko, is that you? What are you doing, sneaking in like that? You frightened me," he said. He dropped his bat on the ground and smiled. He was wearing a long cream gown, a crocheted black cap snugly cradled on his bald head, and brown flip-flops which looked like they'd had better days. Silver wisps streaked his strikingly long black beard.

"Khan Sahib, I thought you might have gone by now. We are heading back to Kakira. I thought I'd see if you were still here. Why haven't you left yet?" Miko asked.

"Miko, my friend. These last few weeks have been terrifying. Come inside first. Sit down and rest a moment. I'll tell you everything," he said, walking back towards the mosque.

Inside was an ornate, hand carved, sandalwood shoe rack. Carpentry and woodwork appealed to me. I'd often thought about becoming an apprentice. But being at the garage with my father was probably the best place for me. That way Adha could monitor me when my motivation levels dropped.

We removed our shoes and neatly placed them on the rack.

There were long rows of velvet prayer mats, all facing the direction of the Mihrab, *(an arch on the wall, representing the direction of the Kaaba in Mecca)*. Our local mosque in Kakira had a Mihrab, intricately crafted from mosaic mirrors. I would often sit and admire it after Friday prayers. This one was simpler, but still superbly made.

I traced my fingers over the top of the floral patterns, hand drawn in gold paint against a royal blue background.

"Beautiful, isn't it?" Khan Sahib said from behind me.

"Yes. Did you paint this? It's so perfect," I responded, amazed by the symmetry in the patterning.

"Oh no. My eldest daughter Shahida created this masterpiece. She's a very talented artist. As a child she would draw on walls with chalk. She adores art and illustration," he said with a proud smile. "Come. Just through these doors here," Khan Sahib said, inviting us in.

He took out a key attached to a long cord around his neck, concealed under his gown. Opening the little rusty lock, he led us through a very short wooden door. Proceeding through the creaky, gnome-sized entrance, we entered a small kitchen area. Another human-sized door on the far side led to other rooms in the house.

All three of us sat down around a wooden table. The stools were padded with red patterned cushions. The sequins were sharp, so I turned the cushion over.

"That again is my daughter Shahida's doing. Everything must be patterned with a full set of sharp sequins," he giggled, getting up and grabbing a pan. "Chai?" he asked.

"Yes please. That would be heaven. Can you make it with masala please—like you used to, Khan Sahib?" Miko requested, with a smile.

"You like your masala chai, huh?" I asked Miko.

"This man is more Asian than I am," Khan Sahib chuckled. "You know, Miko cooks the most delicious fish biryani with tilapia," Khan Sahib said, adding spices to the chai.

"Fish biriyani? You're kidding me, right?" I asked, glaring at Miko.

"Yes! Speaking of tilapia, Miko, do you remember those fishing trips at Lake Victoria with only a line, a hook and some bread?" Khan Sahib said, stirring the tea.

"Those days were special. We would always go home with a prize," Miko said with a soft smile.

"Apart from the time when Cecil chased us! Remember him? He was strong, fierce and faster than an angry hornet," Khan Sahib said. They both chuckled.

"Who's Cecil," I asked.

"Cecil, or 'C-Sharp' as Miko called him, was a gigantic crocodile. He ruled the roost and was never to be messed with," Khan Sahib explained.

"Yes! C-Sharp. He was full of scales and razor-sharp teeth," Miko giggled.

Khan Sahib poured out three cups of tea and brought them over to us, before grabbing a large steel container. He popped open the lid and took out a paper bag full of fluffy coconut biscuits. My favourite kind.

"So how do you know each other?" I said, stuffing two biscuits in my mouth at once.

"Amiri, the biscuits are not running away, take your time," Miko laughed.

Crumbs fell as I tried to purse my lips together. With a shrug, I carried on chomping. The biscuits were heavenly.

"Miko and I have been buddies for the last twenty-eight or twenty-nine years. We used to be neighbours in Kakira. I moved ten years ago to this mosque," he said, pouring his tea into his saucer and slurping it from the rim, just like Adha, when he was in the company of friends.

"Neighbours? That means you must know my father!" I said in excitement.

"Who is your father?" he enquired.

"Ismail Adam Majothi," I said nervously. It felt unusual reciting my father's name.

"Ismail bhai! Of course I know him. I met him for the first time when you moved to Kakira from Iganga. You were only a little boy then. Gosh, you've grown incredibly tall like your father. Mashallah!" he exclaimed. *(Mashallah is a term often used by Muslims to express joy, praise or appreciation in the name of God).*

"My family left for Britain a few weeks back. I needed to get my passport issued," I said, taking another biscuit from the tin.

"Khan Sahib, I took Amiri and a few other local passengers earlier this week to Kakira, but on the way we got lost and ended up in Amin's army barracks and—"

"Ya Allah! How did you get out alive? I hope you kept your mouth shut about Obote. Honestly, Miko. You have to be careful now!" Khan Sahib interjected, clearly familiar with Miko's political views and expressive personality.

"Let's just say we were lucky to leave. They held guns to us. We thought that was it. And yes, I kept my mouth shut. I love Obote, but my life is precious too," Miko said, finally helping himself to the biscuits.

"These are harsh times. I sent my wife and three daughters away last month. They've flown to Canada, and I hope to follow them soon. My wife is a nurse along with my youngest daughter. I sent them as quickly as possible after a terrifying incident," Khan Sahib said, looking down at his teacup.

"What happened, dear brother?" Miko asked, his eyes

troubled.

Khan Sahib took a sip of his chai. "Soldiers broke through the gates in an army vehicle and started firing shots in the air. My wife and I ran outside to see what the fuss was about, along with twelve other men inside, who had arrived for prayers. We gathered outside in union, shoulder to shoulder, but terrified to our core. That's when we saw four soldiers jump out of their vehicle," he sighed. "I asked them what they wanted, and they exclaimed that they had arrived to take charge of the building. I knew that this was inevitable, but I tried reasoning with them, explaining that we still had time until our deadline. They ignored me and barged through into the mosque making their way into my house. I chased them and demanded that they leave. They took our black and white television along with our radio. My youngest daughter dashed over to see what was happening. She stood still, frightened from the sight of the soldier with his gun. He approached her and snatched a gold necklace from her neck. My wife, Nazeera and I had bought that necklace for her sixteenth birthday. The way he looked at my daughter was enough to make me want to destroy every bone in his body. He whispered to the other soldier, that they would come back for the '*rest*', with a sickening smile. That was when I knew I had to get my girls out of here, fast."

A moment of silence filled the air around us. Miko and I took that moment to process what we had heard. Another seed of detachment, from what I thought was my motherland, had been sown.

"I leave tomorrow, I can't stay here any longer either. Most of my belongings are packed. My brother's also here. We'll be travelling to the airport together," Khan Sahib said, finishing his tea.

"Khan Sahib, I'm so sorry to hear that. You did the right thing by getting the women out of here first," Miko said, with his arm on Khan Sahib's shoulder.

"Miko, this is no longer home now. This is terror," he said, shaking his head.

We bid Khan Sahib farewell in the front yard. It felt soothing to meet someone who knew my family. Khan Sahib was a warm and welcoming man with a big heart. It was charming to see a devout Christian and a Muslim Imam embracing one another, like brothers. Ugandan villages were populated with Hindus, Muslims, Sikhs and Christians, living in harmony, enjoying one another's festivals and cultures. I couldn't help but wonder if my new homeland would be the same.

"Miko, we may never meet again, but may Allah always be with you, my brother. Stay safe in Uganda and stay out of trouble," Khan Sahib said with a smile, before hugging Miko one more time.

"And may Jesus be with you, Khan Sahib. Don't be eating too much sugar in Canada. Look after your health and your family," Miko said, parting ways.

Within the hour we were back in Kakira, back to dealing with reality—back to kismet.

CHAPTER NINETEEN

1964 - Kakira, Uganda
Age 11

"But why can't I come and play with you?" Kabir cried.

"Because you're six and I'm eleven. You're a baby! My friends don't want to play with *you*," I shouted, becoming more and more irate with my little brother's whining.

"Which friend said that? They all like me. You're lying to me," Kabir yelled, wiping away more tears.

"Harman thinks you're a headache. Kimo's also bored of babysitting you. Just stay at home and don't follow me. Do you understand?" I barked.

"What on earth is all this bickering about?" Maa said, peering out from behind our bedroom door.

"Amir won't let me play outside with him, Maa."

This was becoming a weekly affair. Kabir would frequently get his way and end up tagging along. But I was determined to leave the house alone.

"Just take him along, he gets bored at home," Maa said.

"Maa no! He's a liability. Last time he nearly got run over. He never watches the road. I don't want to be held responsible if he gets hurt," I said, my palms together as I pleaded.

"Ok, Kabir, come on. I will take you with me today," Maa said in a patronising tone.

"Where are we going, Maa?" he asked, taking a momentary pause from wailing.

"To the back yard. I'm planting lots of new vegetables today. You can come and be my star planting hero," Maa said smiling, obviously hoping he would bite.

"Maa, I want to go out with Amir, not just to the backyard," he cried, before climbing onto the top bunk and resentfully burying his head under his pillow.

"Ok I have to go now," I chirped, grabbing my football.

"Don't be too late. Take some jambus with you from the kitchen," Maa said, as I passed her.

My pockets would always be full of juicy jambus for snacking on after the game.

A few streets away, building work was underway. New homes were being erected, and much of the ground had been dug up in preparation. On weekends, the site was fairly derelict with not a single builder or labourer in sight. Kimo, Harman, Niraj and I figured we could climb down into one of the vast foundation pits and have a quick game of football. We liked the idea of being able to kick the ball as hard as possible without losing it in a field or yard. The pit was perfect.

The labourers had left a wooden ladder by the side of the pit and we used this to climb down, as it was at least twelve or thirteen feet deep.

"I don't know about this," Kimo said, peering down from the top of the ladder.

"Come on, Kimo, let's get down there. No one can disturb us, and the ball will stay with us. Stop being a chicken," I gibed.

"Fine. But if something happens, don't say I didn't warn you all," Kimo moaned, reluctantly climbing down.

We got off to a grand start. Niraj and Kimo played

against Harman and me.

"Goal!" I shouted, followed by an impromptu Bollywood victory dance.

"Oh wow! Dev Anand scores the first goal," shouted Harman, running towards me.

As I turned to give him a celebratory high five, I felt a sharp blow to my head. My knees buckled, and I dropped to the ground. My eyes were still wide open, my vision distorted. Black spots were circulating, with other hazy shapes. I heard Harman's voice echo, "Look up there. It's Kabir. Get him."

Niraj's voice then sounded, "Look at all those jambus on the floor! Get them!"

For a moment, I experienced numbness, followed by dreadful pains. It felt as if my head had been cracked open.

"Miah! Miah! Can you hear me? Get up, get up," Harman gasped.

"Harman—what—what the hell happened?" I slurred, holding my head in my hands, worried that my brains had spilled out.

"It was Kabir, I saw him before he bolted off. He threw a rock—no—a boulder on your head, and ran," Harman bleated.

My hands felt moist. It was blood.

The boys helped me up and supported my body weight, whilst climbing the ladder.

"Push guys, or I'll fall. I feel dizzy," I panted, nearing the top of the ladder.

"We are trying, Miah. Kimo you push too, I can't hold all the weight," Harman said, holding me up from behind, with Kimo right behind him.

"I would, but Niraj isn't helping me. He's still stuffing

his face on Miah's jambus," Kimo shouted.

"What? No, I'm not," Niraj asserted, with his mouth full.

Once the boys got me home, Maa and Johari came darting into the hallway.

"What is this! What happened? Ya Allah! Why is there blood all over you, child?" Maa cried. Johari bolted into the kitchen, returning with a first aid box.

"We were playing football in the housing pits, Aunty. Then Kabir turned up. He threw a rock on Amir's head and ran away," Harman said.

It was the first time I'd heard him use my actual name in years.

"What?" Maa was confused. I watched as the cloud of confusion on her face dispersed and was replaced by seething, thunderous anger. This look was far worse than the Indian death stare. I'd only ever witnessed it once before, when my older brother Aziz had broken Maa's porcelain serving dish. A wedding gift to her from her late father. She never let him forget what an atrocity he'd carried out that day.

Maa was ready to go into the battlefield once again, armed with her leather slipper.

"Kabir!" she snarled. "Come here now. Where are you?" she shouted once more.

She was on the prowl, an angry lioness hunting her prey.

Johari had mopped up all the excess blood and put a makeshift bandage in place. "The wound is deep, Jilu, we need to call the doctor or take him to the hospital. He will need stitches I'm afraid," Johari said, disposing of the blood-stained rags.

"Stitches!" I yelled, "I'm not having stitches. I can't believe what that little brat has done. It's all his fault," I whimpered, dizzy from the thought of a needle and thread sewing up my head.

"Kabir. Come out NOW!" Maa blared at the top of her voice.

"Maa let's go and check if he's in the bedroom," I said, suspecting that he may have hidden in there.

Maa followed me in, only to find Kabir with his head pushed under the bunk bed, with his bottom sticking out in the air.

"Kabir, you're in trouble," I chirped with a cocky grin. He remained still and quiet, like an Ostrich, unaware that we could see him.

"We can see you hiding under the bed, you silly boy," Maa said, before giving him a sharp smack on his bottom with her slipper.

"Aagh!" Kabir cried, rubbing his posterior. He got up and ran towards Maa's bedroom with zero eye contact. Puzzled, we followed him in.

"Kabir, come here now! You've got some answering to do," Maa exclaimed.

He squeezed his head under the bed. His bottom was sticking out once again. Johari and I couldn't help but chortle.

"Kabir, we can see you, including your butt. Get ready for another one," I said, before Maa dispensed another sharp smack.

"Maa! No. I'm sorry," Kabir cried, once again clutching his rear. Maa slid him out from under her bed and sat him on top.

"Why did you do that? Why did you hurt your brother? Do you realise how dangerous that was? A huge rock like that could have killed him?" Maa screamed.

"It wasn't supposed to land on Amir. It was meant to land on Harman. He's the one who never wants me to come out and play with them," Kabir cried, wiping floods of tears from his muddy face.

"That's no excuse. Look what's happened to your brother. He needs stitches because of you. Apologise right now," Maa said, still fuming.

I'd briefly forgotten about the gaping wound. Resentment came cascading back.

"Maa we have to tell Adha what he's done. He'll be in deeper trouble then. Grounded for weeks," I said, with a smirk.

"No please, Maa, don't tell Adha. I'll do anything you say," Kabir cried, with increasing volume.

"Your father will deal with you. Just wait till he gets home today, you'll see," Maa said, throwing her slipper down.

"He won't be able to see anything, Maa. His head will be under the bed again, with his butt sticking out," I laughed.

"Stop cackling like a hyena. Johari will take you to get your stitches. Get on with it! If you would have listened to me in the first place, and taken him with you, this would never have happened. I don't know what to do with you boys!" Maa exclaimed, ushering us out of her room.

CHAPTER TWENTY

22nd October 1972 - Kakira, Uganda
Age 19

"Tito," I shouted, standing at the front door.

Tito took off his gloves and made his way towards me from the neighbour's porch, patting down his clothes.

"Amiri, are you ok?" he asked.

"Tito, come inside. I've made a piping hot cup of chai for you. Take a break from all the bags and cases. I wanted to speak to you about something important," I said nervously.

Tito gave me a nod, and we sat down in the living room. For the first time, I'd used a coaster underneath my cup. Whenever Maa would see me putting anything onto her precious coffee table, she'd always jump in and shout *'use a coaster please.'* No one ever did.

"Tito, I need to talk to you about the house and about Rocky," I said, before taking a deep breath.

"Okay, Amiri, go ahead," he said.

I lightly pressed my thumb against the edge of the coaster before proceeding.

"I know what your plans are, Tito, but I really want you to have this house. It's everything my parents have ever worked for and you've helped to look after it for so many years with your mother. Keep this place. Keep it and look after it. Please," I said, looking into his eyes.

"Amiri—that is so kind, but—"

"I know what you will say," I interrupted. "But this is your home too. We can get some paperwork done now before I leave, so they register you as the proprietor. What do you think?" I said, hoping he would take the offer.

"Amiri. I can't stay in Uganda. My mother is already in Kenya, waiting for me to come back to her. I've promised her I'll come as soon as I've seen you off. I'm so honoured that you're giving me everything you own. But, Amiri, it's too dangerous for me to stay behind," Tito said.

Memories of Obote's soldiers, storming our home, came flooding back. He was right. Amin's soldiers would surely target non-Ugandan citizens as soon as the Asians left. It was inevitable.

"You're right. I'm sorry, brother, I haven't thought this through properly. Be with your mother and family," I said, placing my hand on his shoulder. "Can I ask you for an alternative favour? Take any possessions you wish from this house. Pack everything you can carry. Take anything your mother may like from the kitchen cupboards. At least she'll be able to use and look after Maa's things."

"No problem. With your permission, I'll take whatever I can manage," Tito said, smiling back at me. "Thank you, Amiri. I'm just so sorry this is happening to you. To us," he said, gazing at the floor.

"I must find Rocky a home. I can't just abandon him here. He needs a family. What should I do, Tito?" I asked, miserable from the thought of having to let him go.

"Amiri, don't worry, I know a few families who can help. There's always Miko. He loves Rocky, and Rocky knows him," Tito said.

"That's true. I could ask him to take the house too. He may be able to take the property papers," I said, feeling hopeful.

"Amiri, what about the garage? What did your father do with it?"

"Adha handed it over to Akello, our youngest garage worker. We know him well. He's supported his grandparents ever since his father passed away."

"At least it's gone to someone deserving, Amiri. Your father is a good man. I miss him so much already," Tito said, resting his head in his hands.

"Me too, Tito. Me too."

CHAPTER TWENTY-ONE
1964 - Kakira, Uganda
Age 11

The sound of applause filled the assembly hall. It was our end-of-year 'Prize Day' ceremony. I specifically loathed this day. It was a day for children like Sarita, who spent their entire school year as prefects, to obtain their rewards. Rolling my eyes, I would clap, like a sloth, barely bringing my palms together, with my head tilted to one side, ready to doze off.

One after the other, children were making their way to the stage to collect their prizes in various categories. There were prizes in Maths, English, Science, reading, writing, and of course, the Student of the Year Award.

Sarita had won this award for every year that I could remember. She would bore the audience with mindless speeches about setting outstanding examples and being a good role model.

"And this year's Student of the Year Award goes to none other than Sarita Neha Aggarwal," announced the headmaster. Applause filled the hall once again.

Sarita was perched on a bench directly in front of where Kimo and I were sitting in the assembly hall. She stood up and acknowledged the crowd with a fake smile. Sarita then glanced back at Kimo and I, pulling a horrid face, before leaving to go on stage.

"The little witch. She thinks she's so smart. One day

I'll get hold of her tiffin and fill it with dog poo. Just wait!" Kimo whispered.

"Kimo, that's crazy," I laughed. "And disgusting. I'll help you," I said, holding my hand over my mouth whilst we giggled. "Oh no, here we go. She's on stage now," I said, tilting my head again, losing the will to live.

"I would like to thank all my amazing teachers for helping me to become better at school every year. Without you amazing people in my life guiding me, I wouldn't be the perfect student that I am. But most of the credit does go to my own hard work and dedication," Sarita proclaimed.

The teachers were raising their eyebrows at one another. I could see the amusement on their faces. I couldn't believe her arrogance.

"Anyway, thank you again for this award. I look forward to winning again next year. I would now like to say a few words about my journey. Firstly, I would like to—"

"I think that's all we've got time for, Sarita. Let's move on to the award for literacy skills," the headmaster interrupted, before shuffling her off stage.

Another round of applause followed. Sarita obviously thought it was for her; however, we were just happy to see her escorted away. She sat back down on the bench in front of Kimo and I, stroking the multicoloured satin ribbons on either side of her golden trophy.

The trophy cup was mounted on a piece of wood with a metal plate. Her name was etched on in bold text. She sat tracing her fingers across the nameplate for a few minutes, before Kimo became irate and pulled her plait from behind.

"Ouch," Sarita yelled.

A teacher at the side of our row leaned forward and

hushed her.

"How dare you," she hissed, turning around and looking right at me.

"What? I didn't even do anything," I said, trying my best not to glance at Kimo, and give his game away.

"You pulled my hair. You're just jealous," she spat.

"Why on earth would I be jealous of a teacher's pet monkey like you?" I spouted back.

"Aww, poor Amir will never get an award. Unless they give awards for being hooligans or having abnormal ribs. You'll get first prize then. What's actually wrong with your ribs? Why do they stick out? You freak of nature," she said, before turning back around.

"You witch! There's nothing wrong with my ribs!" I growled, crossing my arms to shield my chest from the gaze of the other children. She had gone too far. No-one ever spoke about my ribcage or asked why it was misshapen.

"If she labels me a hooligan, I'll be a hooligan," I whispered to myself, before yanking on her plait twice as hard as Kimo had done.

The entire hair piece came off into my hands, along with the little red ribbon tied on the end.

Sarita screamed.

I tossed the hair piece into Kimo's satchel, open on the floor.

"Miah, what are you doing? If they search my bag, I'm a goner. Why did you pull it so hard?" Kimo whispered, sounding panicked.

"Don't worry, just trust me. I'll get it out. I'll think of something. I'm sorry. Just keep cool for now and deny everything," I said, composing myself.

The headmaster came storming off the stage towards

us. Sarita stood up on her bench and began pointing her finger at us, stamping her foot like a spoilt brat.

"Sarita, get down from the bench," the headmaster raged.

She wasn't expecting that.

"But Sir, these two just pulled off my plait."

"Be quiet," he shouted.

I smirked at Sarita.

"Don't start feeling so smug about yourself, Amir. What did you do? Where is Sarita's hair piece? How dare you kids ruin this ceremony," he said, his arms folded in a tight lock.

"It wasn't me, Sir. It could have been anyone, but we didn't see anything at all. We just saw Sarita stand up and scream for no reason, Sir," I said, hoping he would remain impartial.

"Right, we will check all the pockets and bags of students seated in this row," he snapped, looking at his colleagues at each side. "Let's start on the ends," he said, nodding to the teachers.

"Miah, I'm going to be dead meat. Get me out of this mess you've gotten me into," Kimo whispered, pleading for me to help.

Sarita had made her way to the far left of our row, to assist the teachers in the bag inspection, like a little madam. To my delight, I noticed her bag was left wide open under her seat. That was my opportune moment.

Sarita's friend Geeta shuffled over into Sarita's seat. The moment had gone.

"Miah do something, please!" Kimo whispered.

"Kimo, just hold on. I was going to put it into Sarita's bag, but now Geeta is there. Try to distract her," I said.

Kimo immediately leaned over to Geeta.

"Hi, Geeta. So, are you up for an award today?" Kimo said with a nervous smile.

"Kimo be quiet. I don't have time for boys like you," she said in a pompous tone, before turning away.

"I know you don't like me, but I really believe that you should have got that award this year, not Sarita," Kimo said. I gave him a puzzled look. He returned a wink.

"Really, Kimo? And why is that?" she asked with a sigh.

"Well, if you think about it, it's you who does all the hard work. You're the one who comes up with the grand ideas and Sarita claims them as her own. Do you get any recognition? No. And how many times have you done all the legwork in arranging sports day activities? In the end, who takes credit and bores everyone with her speech? That's right—Sarita," he said.

Kimo continued to distract Geeta. She was finally beginning to smile a little and had turned the other way to face Kimo with her back to me, curling little tufts of her hair around her fingers.

"So, do you think I should have got it? Do you think I'm a better student?" she asked with a twinkle in her eyes, fully engrossed.

Kimo gave her another nervous smile. Even I was confused by her sudden warm attitude.

"Oh, yes—erm yes. You definitely should have won. Everyone in the school knows that," Kimo said.

"Oh, you're so sweet," Geeta said, placing her hand on Kimo's hand.

My eyeballs nearly popped out of their sockets, and I almost burst out into a fit of laughter. Instead, I curbed any knee-jerk reactions and swiftly tossed the hairpiece from Kimo's bag into Sarita's satchel.

Thankfully it was only Kimo who'd spotted what I'd done and let out a tremendous sigh of relief. I watched as he became aware that Geeta had clasped his hand in hers.

"So, it's a shame Sarita got it this year. Better luck next year, loser!" he yelled in her face before abruptly snatching his hand away.

"You dog!" Geeta yelled.

Kimo and I howled like wolves.

"Kimo, you're too funny," I giggled.

"I learnt from you, Miah," he laughed.

They had checked all the bags. Kimo's bag was thoroughly inspected, along with mine.

"Sarita, we have checked everyone's bags and pockets. No one has your hairpiece. Nor did anyone see what happened," the headmaster said, placing his hands on his hips.

"Sir, no one has checked Sarita's bag. I bet this is another one of her plans to get us into trouble. She does this every time," I said.

"My bag? Why would it be in my bag? You're the one who pulled my hair, I know it," she yelled, stamping both of her feet on the ground.

"Enough! Both of you. Sarita, pass me your bag and let me check," ordered the headmaster.

"With pleasure, Sir," she said, sneering at us.

Within seconds the headmaster pulled out her hairpiece.

"Is this what you're looking for, young lady?" he said, dangling it in the air with fire in his eyes.

"She's doomed," Kimo whispered, trying to hold himself together.

"Yup. An additional complimentary prize," I said, feeling rather smug.

The assembly hall filled with a mixture of laughter, shock and booing. One student shouted, "She's always trying to be the centre of attention."

Another voice yelled, "She needs to be suspended. She would demand the same if someone actually pulled her plait out. She always gets her own way. Spoilt brat."

"That's enough, children. Sarita, you're coming with me. The rest of you go back to your classroom. The ceremony is on hold and will continue tomorrow. Sarita—march—now," he raged.

"But, Sir, it wasn't—"

"NOW!" he snapped, his gaze sharply locked on her, his hand stiffly pointing to the doors.

Later that day, word spread through the school that Sarita was told to stay behind after lessons to clean all the classrooms. She was to continue every day after school until all desks were gleaming, free of chewing gum underneath, and washed clean of any graffiti marks. Kimo and I were overjoyed. So were the rest of the pupils. Possibly even some staff members.

CHAPTER TWENTY-TWO
23rd October 1972 - Kakira, Uganda
Age 19

For the third time, I pounded my fists on Miko's front door.

"Coming. Hold on," came Miko's voice. He finally opened the door.

"Ah, Amiri. You've brought Rocky along with you too. How are you?" Miko said, rubbing Rocky's chin.

"Sorry, Miko, I didn't mean to knock so hard. It worried me when you didn't answer straight away. I guess I'm just—"

"It's ok, Amiri. Don't panic. Come inside. Bring my friend Rocky inside too," he said, waving for us to follow.

We sat down on his luxurious leather settee. Miko's house was quite lavishly furnished compared to the rest of the homes on the street. His television looked to be brand new and his radio was classy and ornate. Black and white family portraits adorned his walls, encased in decorative mahogany frames of all shapes and sizes.

"Amiri, let me get you some juice," he said, getting up from the settee.

"No, Miko. I came to discuss something very important with you," I said, extending my arm, signalling for him to stay. He sat back down.

"Amiri, what is it?" he asked, looking at me questioningly.

"You need to take the house. My home. We have to transfer the paperwork to you before my uncle and I leave," I said.

"But, Amiri, you can't be thinking about these things now. You've got your passport. You need to leave quickly. It's becoming more and more dangerous for you to stay as we get closer to the deadline. You know there are only seventeen days remaining? God forbid if something happens to you now after everything you've gone through."

"Miko, I know. But my parents have worked so hard for it. Miko, please take it. Before the soldiers do," I pleaded.

"Amiri, if that is what you wish, that's fine. We can do this. But you shouldn't be wasting time. What about Rocky?" Miko asked.

"Well, I was hoping—"

"Of course. He's already my friend. Leave him with me," Miko said, patting Rocky on the head.

"Really? Oh, Miko, thank you. You don't know what this means to me," I gasped, squeezing him against my chest.

"Oh, Amiri. Don't worry. I appreciate what you're giving me."

"I just can't leave my home knowing it could get seized by Amin's soldiers. At least this way it will be with you, our friend," I said, dropping my shoulders in relief.

A look of uncertainty flashed across Miko's eyes.

"Amiri, you know, if they want to take it, then they will. They're capable of anything. I can't promise your home will be in safe hands forever. But I will do my best."

"That's all I ask. At least I'll feel like I tried."

"Ok, so tomorrow we can go to Kampala to arrange the property documents. You must come with me," he said, with a hint of a smile.

"As long as you don't get us lost again, Miko," I chuckled.

Although the thought of another road trip with Miko made me question my proposition.

That night I played with Rocky in my backyard. I couldn't help but feel sorrow in my heart, having to leave him behind. *If only there was a way to take him with me,* I thought. But I'd heard they weren't allowing dogs. Apparently, some families had taken their African Grey parrots with them. I wondered how such small and delicate creatures would survive the journey. Perhaps they didn't. Rocky was my little baby. He was too gentle to be anyone's guard dog. Knowing that someone as caring as Miko would look after him was a relief. It comforted me knowing that he'd be safe, and that our home would be protected from being pillaged.

"Amir, come inside now. It's getting late. Come and eat something," Uncle Usman called from the back door.

Making my way inside, it suddenly hit me that my days and hours were numbered. It really was time to go. There wasn't much left for me to do. Everything was almost taken care of.

Closing the door behind me, I bolted the top and bottom locks. Uncle Usman was loitering in the hallway holding a newspaper, glaring at the front page. I could sense his frustration as he flicked the pages. He was frowning so hard his brows seemed almost to meet in the middle.

"Uncle? What's wrong?" I asked, curious about the latest delights of the Uganda Argus.

"We need to move fast. It's not safe anymore," he said, closing the paper and swatting it into the palm of his hand. "There are check posts on the way to the airport, at every step. Soldiers know there are thousands of Asians making their way out of the country. They are robbing them of their possessions at these posts. We have to be clever about how we pack certain things, like money and gold," he said, scratching his head.

"I only have money and my watch that Adha gave me for my birthday. Apart from that, I'm taking my clothes and a blanket. Maa took any gold she had, which wasn't much. What do you suggest we do?" I asked.

"Hmm—bring me the shoes you'll wear on the day, along with your trousers and jacket," he said, still rubbing his crown.

"Are you going to—"

"Yes. I know for sure they'll take what's in our wallets. If not at the check posts, then at the airports," he said, getting up and walking towards the television cabinet. He pulled out a small toolbox, along with a pair of pliers and a tube of superglue.

He cut into the sole of my shoes using a sharp blade. The sole came apart seamlessly. I was quite impressed with his neat handiwork. Inside the soles were hollow cavities.

"Right, bring all the money your father has left you. We will stuff as much as possible in both shoes and glue the soles back in place," he said.

It was like a scene from a Hollywood film, smuggling possessions via my shoes, with the help of an accomplice.

"What about my watch? Will that fit in my soles?" I asked, removing it from my wrist.

"No. That won't fit at all. We can sew that inside the

collar of your jacket with a little padding to mask its shape."

It felt thrilling to know we were hiding things within our shoes and clothes. But then again, these were *our* things. Our possessions, which we had a right to own and keep. This was the only way we had a chance at taking a tiny fraction of our belongings and memories out of the country with us.

We spent the night sewing, gluing and hiding whatever we could manage.

Uncle Usman even had a small gold chain that belonged to his wife, which he stowed away in the handle of his suitcase, perfectly glued back together. I remember thinking that was just pure genius. The soldiers would never think to look inside there.

"Make sure you leave enough money in your pockets too. If you hide everything, they'll get suspicious. Leave some in your wallet and maybe a little inside your socks to give to airport security. They'll be expecting it," Uncle Usman said, sealing the last part of the sole over his brown leather shoes.

CHAPTER TWENTY-THREE
1961 - Kakira, Uganda
Age 8

"But why does she have to go?" I cried out.

"She has to go with her husband now, Amir. Stop whining today of all days, for heaven's sake. It's your Aunty Mumtaz's wedding day. Now wash your hands, they're sticky from all the jam and coconut biscuits you've been stuffing yourself with. Don't even think about wiping them on your white shirt. If I find you've made it dirty, you'll be in big trouble. Do you understand?" Maa lectured, dragging me over to the kitchen sink.

"Yes Maa," I muttered, scrubbing my hands with soap, standing on my tiptoes to reach the taps.

"Now dry your hands, go outside in the marquee and help Aziz and your father see to the guests. Off you go," she said, before shoving me out of the kitchen. As I passed my bedroom door, I thought about grabbing my sunglasses and handkerchief to put on a small Bollywood dance show for the guests, but reconsidered at the thought of Maa's slipper.

The marquee had at least sixty to seventy guests sitting underneath it, on brightly coloured cushions. It was propped up in the middle of our street. But it didn't seem to matter as we lived at the end of the road in what would be best described as a cul-de-sac. Hardly any cars would come all the way up to us. It seemed to be the same marquee and same cushions at all weddings within the village. I also recognised the large and boisterous singing lady who was hammering her spoon on the dholki drum whilst belting out a very painful, unmelodious wail.

Unsure what to think of all the commotion, I stood glaring at her and all the other ladies singing beside her. They all sat on the floor in a circle, surrounding the dholki, clapping their hands. They must have noticed the look of disgust on my face because the music stopped, followed by the singing.

"What's the matter, little boy? Don't you like our songs?" one lady asked.

"The songs are great. The singers, not so much. Something missing here," I answered, with a hint of cockiness.

The crowds had locked their gaze on me. I glanced to the back of the marquee and spotted my Aunty Mumtaz perched on a posh chair beside her groom. She was adorned in a red and gold sari, with her hands covered in henna patterns. Her eyes widened, pleading for me to disappear.

"Oh! So you think you can entertain a crowd better than us then? Can you tell us what this missing *something* is, please?" jibed another lady.

"Yes. It's called style, baby," I said, blowing her a kiss and giving her a wink.

The guests roared with laughter.

"He's certainly got style, I'll give him that," one of the gentlemen exclaimed.

"Okay, young one. Show us what you've got if you're brave enough," the large singing lady said, proposing a challenge I was most ready for.

"Fine. I'll be back with my props," I said, before bolting into the house, heading straight for my bedroom. I grabbed my plastic Ukulele, which didn't function at all. It was just a toy with plastic strings. I dipped my hand into the water jug Maa kept on my dresser and slicked my hair down to one side. I threw on my sunglasses and tied my purple handkerchief around my neck before darting back outside.

"He's back! Let's see what he's got for us," one of the ladies chimed.

Holding my Ukulele by the neck, I swung it over my shoulder and pushed my sunglasses down to the tip of my nose.

"I may be young, but I do no wrong. I'm braver than the mighty hero, Dev Anand. Now please may I have silence. Hear my song," I recited, before jumping in the air and down to my knees, striking the non-active strings on my fake instrument. It was followed by a verbal "Pow," as if I was striking an electric guitar.

The crowd applauded, making their way closer to where I was standing. I caught a glimpse of my Aunty Mumtaz slowly sinking into her chair, covering her face with her veil.

They watched me burst out into song and dance, copying Dev Anand's every move from a song I'd become obsessed with. The song was taken from his Bollywood hit, *'Jab Pyaar Kisi Se Hota Hai.'*

"Yeh aanken, uff yummah. Yeh soorat, uff yummah. Pyar kyoon na hoga? Yeh adaayein, uff yummah!"
(These eyes, oh my. This face, oh my. How can one not fall in love? Your style and grace, oh my!)

Applause had filled the marquee. For a moment, I was Dev Anand himself, the shining superstar, applauded by his adoring fans. That star-studded moment didn't last long.

A burning sensation took over my ear. Fingers were tightly pressed against my earlobe, twisting it full circle.

"Maa! I'm only being Dev Anand," I cried.

"You're being a clown and a nuisance. Get inside right now and help Aziz take out the drinks. Stop making a fool of yourself and let the ladies carry on with their songs," Maa hissed, whilst escorting me back inside, her fingers almost tearing my ear away from my head. She was furious, so I knew my talent show was over. No chance of a sequel.

Unwilling to ditch my sunglasses, I served guests with watered down fruit juice. Maa was frugal when catering for large numbers. She was shrewd at bartering and haggling over the lowest possible prices for food and drinks in the markets. She would use plenty of potatoes and peas to fill the samosas, with very meagre amounts of mincemeat. Her chicken kebabs on little skewers had more veg than meat on them. The loose tea was re-boiled a few times before being replaced with fresh leaves and the drinks were consistently watered down. Maa would add a little sugar to the mix if the juice was over diluted. She was thrifty, but a clever woman who knew how to make a little go a long way.

Taking my tray of sugar water in the tiniest cups, made for elves, I headed outside towards a crowd of gentlemen huddled together, smoking cigarettes and pipes, discussing politics.

"Well, he was the one responsible for splitting the Ugandan National Congress party into two groups. The group led by Obote has now joined forces with Uganda People's Union party. I bet he's setting himself up for Presidency, just watch and see," one of the men said, puffing on his cigarette.

"I've heard Milton Obote is a good man. He will look after us Ugandan Asians, even if he does come to power, I'm sure of it," came another voice.

After dispensing a few drinks to the men, I made my way over to the group of singing ladies. Feedback on my performance was important to me. Curiosity, mostly.

"Here you go ladies. Some nice refreshments to keep you quiet for a bit longer," I said with a grin.

"You really are a cheeky one, aren't you?" the large singing lady chirped, helping herself to a drink from my tray.

"I'm not cheeky. I'm just me. Talented, me."

"You're Jilu's son. No wonder. You're as full of yourself as she is," the large lady chimed, cackling with her pack of hyenas.

Feelings of rage engulfed me. *How dare they mock my mother?*

"Shehnaz you're terrible," said one of the pack members, giggling to herself.

I think Shehnaz needs to be taught a lesson, I decided.

"Ladies I'll be right back. I'm going to fetch you a nice platter of yummy food. Wait here," I said, with a smirk.

"Yes dear, go bring us a platter from the kitchen. We haven't eaten all day. That's a good boy," Shehnaz said.

"Could have fooled me," I whispered to myself before stepping away.

"What was that?" Shehnaz questioned.
"Oh nothing. I just said, I'll bring the biggest platter."

In the kitchen, Maa, Johari and the neighbours were helping with serving duties. I thought long and hard about how to teach the horrid woman a lesson. There were plenty of trays lined with goodies. The meat platters looked particularly mouth-watering, with juicy kebabs arranged in neat rows.

Those women aren't worthy of being served any food, they need to be served something else, I thought.

Carefully dodging more bodies marching in and out of the kitchen, I made my way out of the back door, into the yard. The sound of Oscar playing with Lalit caught my attention.

"That's it!" I yelled and ran through the connecting gates over to Lalit.

"Lalit! Are you not joining the wedding party?" I asked.

'No. I hate weddings. They're so boring. Nothing fun ever happens and all the Aunties pull my cheeks," he said, throwing his stick again for Oscar to fetch.

"Look, I'm going to get straight to the point. I need to borrow Oscar. Just for five minutes."

"Why? Why do you need Oscar?" Lalit asked, looking perplexed.

"Well. Let's just say, there's a horrible Aunty who needs to be taught a lesson and I'm guessing she doesn't like dogs, like most Aunties around here."

"Amir, no way—you're not going to make a scene, are you? Don't get me into trouble," Lalit pleaded.

"Lalit, I'll take full responsibility, I promise. Just five minutes."

"Fine. Take him. Can I watch? I have a feeling this is going to be crazy," Lalit said.

"Of course. Come and see my talent show, part two!" I laughed.

Taking Oscar by his lead, along with Lalit, I led them to the side of my house under the shade of Maa's mango tree.

"Stay here with Oscar. I'll be back in a second."

"Where are you going now, Amir?"

"I need to sneak something out of the kitchen. Just wait here and keep Oscar hidden."

After making my way back into the kitchen, my next task was to smuggle out the meat platter. Within seconds I found myself able to snatch my target off the worktop and join Lalit and Oscar again outside, without anyone seeing a thing.

"Amir, are you going to—"

"Yup! It's time Oscar had his share of wedding food. He'll be feasting with the hyenas today," I whooped, before charging into battle.

With a tray of kebabs in one hand and Oscar's lead in the other, I darted out into the marquee and emptied the platter all over Shehnaz and the rest of her crew.

"Oscar! Attack," I bellowed.

The ladies looked horrified. The look of terror on their faces when they saw Oscar charging towards them was gratifying.

Screams echoed throughout the tent. Oscar was leaping all over them, digging out the treats from in between where they were all sitting. Kebabs had become entangled in Shehnaz's headscarf. Oscar had gone berserk, rooting through her scarf, whilst Shehnaz was desperately trying to free herself. Her scarf, however, was tightly pinned down to her dress, along with Oscar's claws.

"What on earth is going on here!" Maa screamed, running towards the frantic spectacle. "Oscar! Down boy! Why is Oscar here? What is he doing in the marquee?" Maa yelled again, trying to grasp Oscar's lead.

Shehnaz then managed to stand upright. But within seconds, Oscar had gripped a mouthful of her scarf, with a kebab in there somewhere, tightly locked within his jaws. He pulled it with such brute force that Shehnaz's whole scarf came flying off her head—along with her wig.

"Jilu! Your son is a menace to society. How dare he! Where is my hair piece? Where is it?" Shehnaz shrieked.

Guests were gasping in shock and laughter at the sight of Shehnaz's bald, shiny head on display. Even some of her fellow groupies had trouble containing their amusement.

"I'm so sorry, Shehnaz. I didn't even know you wore one of those. Are you ill or unwell?"

"No, Jilu, I'm not ill. Yes, I wear wigs. A secret that the whole of Kakira now knows, all thanks to your son," Shehnaz yelled.

Lalit casually swooped over, took Oscar's lead and slowly began to creep away.

"Lalit, you stop right there!" Maa said.

"Yes, Aunty Jilu," he replied, his hands trembling.

"Did you bring Oscar here?" Maa asked.

Knowing that the spotlight would shift to me within moments, I decided to make my exit. I began backing up, making my way out from under the marquee. Picking up pace, I withdrew from the crowd.

Turning around, I was about to celebrate my seamless escape, before I felt a heavy grip on my collar, pulling me back.

"Amir. You're coming with me."

It was Adha's voice. The instant feeling of regret swept through the pit of my stomach.

CHAPTER TWENTY-FOUR

26th October 1972 - Kakira, Uganda
Age 19

My suitcase had been neatly tucked under my bed for weeks, I'd often look at it with mixed emotions. The previous night, my uncle had prised open its handles and concealed some money inside before gluing it back together. He only stashed small amounts, but it was better than nothing. This suitcase was my nemesis, and it needed to be conquered. It was chocolate brown, and despite its leathery feel, it was made of thick plastic. After peeling off some loose bits of plastic from the edge of the case, I'd finally plucked up the courage to open it up. A brown and orange chequered pattern lined the inside on a thin layer of silky fabric. I stared at the pattern for some time, before I'd realised I'd zoned out. I'd been thinking of the happier memories with this case; weekends in Jinja, Kampala and road trips to Kenya.

Selecting clothes from my wardrobe, I filled my case with essentials. Three pairs of trousers, three formal pastel shirts, my blue satin Dev Anand shirt, a pair of smart black shoes, a thin blazer, a tie, my favourite collection of movie postcards and my sunglasses. One item I packed with particular care and attention was my wooden elephant. Holding it in the palm of my hand and studying it, as if it was an exhibition piece, I sighed, thinking about the time I'd received it. It was gifted to me by my grandfather. He'd given it to me on the day of the snake bite. I was laid in bed feeling dizzy from the anti-venom injection the village doctor had administered. Having time off from school was a bonus. But I kept looking at the snake bite on my left arm, bursting into tears, and feeling sorry for myself. When my grandfather entered the room, hands hidden behind his back, I knew he'd brought me a gift. That was my cue for erupting in excitement every time. On that occasion he presented me with an ornate wooden carving of an African elephant.

He'd said, *"No matter what happens, you will always have the strength to make it. Find courage and be resilient."*

My little elephant was always comforting to hold, especially when I felt upset or anxious. My grandfather's precious words would come back to me whenever I needed to hear them the most. Placing my beloved carving in my case gave me a surge of motivation and empowerment, allowing me to pick up the pace and finally complete the task at hand. Closing the two clasps on my suitcase, I retired to the edge of my bed, perched like a parrot, inspecting my surroundings. I'd spotted some special items that were destined to be left behind. My trusty guitar, with which I'd spent many nights serenading family and friends after evening meals. A breathtaking oversized painting of the Serengeti hanging on the wall. Aziz's chess set, abandoned to one side. I picked up one of the marble chess pieces, only to realise how incredibly heavy they were; polished to perfection by Adha.

These weren't just things—they were our memories.

The more I pondered over the mass eviction, the more my heart filled with waves of pain and resentment. There was no choice but to accept my fate and the unknown circumstances that lay ahead.

The sun was due to set, and I could no longer delay my next task. For safety reasons, we could only leave the house during daylight hours. Many families had suffered attacks when venturing out at night. I was dreading saying goodbye to Rocky.

Reaching for Rocky's lead hanging on the back-door hooks, I took a deep breath before heading outside. Dusk had set in. The sky was painted shades of burnt orange with highlighted silhouettes of trees. Rocky was in the backyard, busy tearing his teeth into a deflated ball. He released it from his jaws when he caught sight of me and leapt to meet me, propping his paws on my shoulders. He towered over me but would always look directly into my eyes. Holding his face in the palms of my hands, I had so much I needed to say to him. My words wouldn't reach my lips, but I couldn't hold back my tears. Rocky's whimpering made me wonder whether he'd sensed how I was feeling.

"I know you won't understand any of what I'm about to say, but I have to say it. You will have a new home, with an amazing new family. I have to leave this place, Rocky, and I'm never coming back. You'll always be my little tiger. Be good and don't cause any trouble for Miko."

Rocky continued to whimper. Taking his lead, I hesitantly paced with him towards Miko's house. I felt burdened with reluctance and my feet dragged as I walked. I found myself wishing there was someone on the street that I could talk to, just to buy a few more moments of time with Rocky. But there was no one.

Miko's door was in front of me, yet my arms felt too heavy to lift and knock on the door. His door hurled open abruptly.

"Amiri! How are you? I didn't hear you knock. I was just about to head out. Both of you, come in," Miko said with a welcoming smile.

"Miko, I can't stay. If I stay, this will become more difficult than it already is for me," I said. My heart was heavy, my eyes unable to hold the dam bursting its barriers down my cheeks. The muscles in my chin trembled, like that of a young child, parting with a loved one.

"I understand, Amiri. But if you want to see him again before you leave, please come anytime without any hesitation."

"Thank you, Miko. My uncle and I are leaving in the next few days. Thank you for doing this for me. Look after him. He's my baby. I'll leave our house keys with you on the day we depart. It's all down to my uncle and his own paperwork. He's almost ready."

"Amiri, it's my pleasure. Stay safe. Try not to delay things too much now. The quicker you leave, the better."

Miko's was a sincere soul, and I knew Rocky would be happy with him. With this in mind, I handed Rocky's lead to him and left without uttering another word.

"Don't look back. Just don't look back," I whispered to myself.

Later that evening, I sat in the living room, the lights off, lost in thought over Rocky. *Would it have been better if I hadn't brought Rocky home that day and begged Maa to let me keep him? Would he miss me? Or would he forget about me? Would I forget about him? Never.* Rocky was in safe hands and I knew he'd settle in quickly with a familiar, friendly face.

Outside, the moon glowed like a magic orb, casting shadows from the mango trees into the room. A sense of emptiness was in the air and within me. The thought of leaving to be with my family should have filled me with joy, but my heart was still so troubled and anxious.

The door swung open, filling the room with light.

"Whoa! Amir? You frightened me," Uncle Usman gasped, pressing his palm against his chest. "What are you doing in the dark?"

"Sorry. I didn't mean to startle you," I said, briefly making eye contact, before continuing to gaze out of the window.

"Did you take Rocky today?" he asked. I could hear the hesitation in his voice.

"Yes. He's gone," I said, wiping my tears away, reluctant to show my face.

CHAPTER TWENTY-FIVE

1962 - Kakira, Uganda
Age 9

"Aagh! Help me. Someone help me!" came a cry from the backyard.

Aziz was tuning the radio with me in the kitchen, like we did every night after dinner. He leapt up shouting, "Maa? That's Maa's voice."

He sprinted out of the back door shortly followed by Adha, with a torch in hand.

Startled, I went to investigate. Adha's torch cut through the pitch-black night like a samurai sword through a sponge cake, lighting up most of the yard. Maa was bent over, clutching her left hand, wailing in severe pain.

"It's still here somewhere. Be careful it doesn't sting you," Maa cried out, scanning her surroundings.

"Adha, there. Look!" Aziz said, pointing to a pile of deadwood.

Adha focused his torch to reveal a large angry scorpion waving its tail aggressively, ready to strike again.

"Hold the torch, Aziz and don't move from this spot," Adha said, slowly handing the torch over to my brother.

Adha carefully reached for a large plank of wood that lay nearby. Moving slowly to avoid alarming the creature, he stepped to within striking distance, before he lunged forward and struck the scorpion with a sharp blow.

"Adha, did you get it?" I shouted.

He slowly lifted the plank of wood to inspect it.

"Yes. It's dead," he said, his shoulders dropping in relief.

"Adha, what's happening to Maa? Quickly!" Aziz shouted, dropping the torch.

We suddenly realised she was losing consciousness. Adha abandoned the plank and dashed over to her, catching her in time before she dropped to the ground.

"Aziz, run to Doctor Anwar's house and bang on his door as loud as you can. Tell him Maa has been stung by a scorpion and the venom is spreading. Go!" Adha ordered, his arms tightly wrapped around Maa.

Aziz shot past me like a steam train.

"Amir, listen carefully. Go grab your mother's scarf, a towel, or any cloth you can lay your hands on. Go, now," he ordered.

Shaking from fright, my noodle-like legs carried me in through the back door and into the kitchen. Grabbing Maa's rose print scarf hanging on the back of a chair, I ran back out to the yard where Adha was holding her steady. He laid her on the ground and instructed me to bring the torch Aziz had abandoned. Taking Maa's scarf, he hastily tore a lengthy piece from it and tied it securely around her elbow, before scooping her up in his arms and heading back into the house. With the torch still clutched in my tiny sweaty palms, I ventured over to where the scorpion had breathed its last. Taking one slow step at a time with the crackling of dead leaves under my flip-flops, I carefully approached the creature. I had never seen a scorpion before and the light from the torch only enhanced its hair-raising appearance. Four inches away, and armed with a long twig, I got a better view of its grim, freshly disfigured body.

"Boo!" Aziz shouted, pushing my face forward, my nose almost making contact with the lifeless arachnid.

"No!" I shrieked, before dropping the torch, and running into the house sobbing.

Darting into my parents' room, I tried to tell Adha of Aziz's cruel behaviour.

"Amir, go to your room, we don't have time for this right now. Maa is unwell, can't you see?" he said, sounding deeply troubled.

Peering over at the bed, I caught sight of our village doctor administering an oversized injection into Maa's arm, while she lay there, motionless.

"Is Maa going to be ok?" I asked, wiping tears away from my cheeks.

"You did the right thing by tying the cloth. I've drained most of the venom, but some has unfortunately spread. She will suffer from severe fever for the next forty-eight hours while the anti-venom plays its part. After that period has passed, she should be out of danger. Send one of your boys to come and get me if you feel she's getting worse at any point," the doctor said, reaching for his large brown medical bag.

"Thank you so much for coming out so late at night," Adha said, shaking his hand.

Herding me out from the room, Adha ordered me to go to sleep.

I noticed Aziz stood in the hallway with an enormous grin on his face, chuckling to himself.

"Don't worry, you haven't gotten away with that. I'll tell Adha tomorrow about how you scared me. Just you wait," I said, still seething with anger.

"Oh, I'll wait right here. You carry on. Off you go to bed," he said with a snigger.

Turning my nose up at him, I continued to retire to my sanctuary, my haven. Usually Maa would have a laborious task in trying to get me to bed each night and getting me back out of bed on a morning would often require several wrestling moves and a chocolate bribe to get me to the school bus on time. But that night I was worried about her and went without hesitation. Flicking off my flip-flops, trying to toss one in the air higher than the other, I reached for the corner of my blanket and lifted it back.

"Aagh! Adha! Aziz put the dead scorpion in my bed!"

CHAPTER TWENTY-SIX

4th November 1972 - Kakira, Uganda
Age 19

"Amir, get up," came Uncle Usman's voice within my room.

Pulling back my blanket apprehensively, I peered at my surroundings with one eye barely remaining open. My Uncle darted about my room, gathering my belongings.

"What? What's happening?" I muttered, attempting to sit up.

"Bad news. Amin's soldiers have begun looting properties within our area. Many Asians have been burgled and shot. We are four days away from the deadline. No more risks. I'm sending you to Kampala. Now," he said, reaching for my shoes.

"What do you mean by *sending me?* Aren't you coming? I thought we were leaving tomorrow morning, straight for Entebbe airport, together?" I blurted, promptly sitting upright, panicked.

"Miko and I have one more family we have to help this evening. I've made a promise and I can't abandon them now," he said, tucking more money into my shoes.

"When will you be leaving then? And why am I going to Kampala and not Entebbe Airport?"

"There's a hostel in Kampala. Many other Asian families will be there preparing to leave. Mahesh will drop you there today with your belongings. I made a promise to your father that I would make sure you leave Uganda safe and sound. Mahesh will bring me, along with the family I'm helping, early tomorrow morning to the hostel. We'll head out to Entebbe together. I promise."

"But it's not safe for you to stay here alone. What if something happens? I'm scared. You can't stay here another night either," I said adamantly, folding my arms.

"Don't worry about me. After you've left with Mahesh, I'm taking my suitcase, locking up the house and heading over to Miko's place to stay the night with him."

"But you can't—"

"We have no choice, Amir. It's time," he said firmly, handing over my shoes.

"I'll be back in ten minutes. I need to get those padlocks from next door. Hurry and get dressed. Mahesh will be here soon, and Tito is already here, waiting to say goodbye to you," he said, before hastily exiting my room.

Tito! He's leaving for Kenya, I thought, leaping out of bed.

My clothes for the day were already ironed and hanging inside my wardrobe. They were the only items left in there. Unable to take most of our clothing, we had donated it to local Ugandan families in need. Reaching into my wardrobe for the last time, I took hold of a plain white long-sleeved shirt, neatly pressed, a brown tweed blazer with worn down suede elbow patches and a pair of socks. Whilst buttoning up my shirt, I looked around my bedroom, trying to absorb the moment. The sweet smell of the mango tree, whose leaves stroked the window, the uneven rectangular clay tiles that paved the floor in a zigzag, and the wicker lamp shape that was blanketed with dust - so much so, that its original colour was no longer distinguishable. Maa would have been furious with me if she saw how dusty the house had become. But there was no need to clean anymore.

Realising I'd drifted off again, I threw on my shoes and hurried into the living room. There I found Tito patiently waiting.

"Amiri, I've come to say goodbye, my brother." Tito spoke so quietly it could almost have been mistaken for a whisper.

Tito's rucksack was on the floor by his feet, bursting at its seams. There were several objects tied to either side. A pair of grey, tattered trainers that were once brilliant white. A metal tiffin, packed by friendly neighbours, containing snacks for his lengthy journey. There were also some small handmade leather pouches containing more knick-knacks and belongings.

Tito stepped forward and embraced me, letting out a deep sigh.

"Brother Amiri. You have been so kind towards me and my mother. I'll never forget how you saved my life. Look after yourself in your new adventures. Find a nice girl and settle down."

We both grinned.

"Always stay the smiling, cheeky, brave and special person you are," Tito said, slowly pulling away, without making eye contact. He was almost in tears. I already had Murchison Falls gushing down my face.

"Tito, I'll miss you. Look after yourself and your family," I cried out, unable to hide any emotion.

"I'll miss karaoke nights on your guitar. I'll keep practicing my Hindi songs, don't worry," Tito giggled.

"Wait! My guitar," I yelled, before dashing back to my room for a moment, leaving Tito bewildered. "Here, take this with you," I said, gasping from the sprint.

"But this is yours. Amiri I can't—"

"Tito, it's yours now. I won't be able to take it with me. I'd rather you have it than one of the soldiers steal it from me at the airport," I said, pressing for him to take it.

He laid out his palms, and I gently passed him my sweet guitar, like it was a newborn child being passed from one parent to the other. With one hand supporting the body and the other the neck, Tito took the guitar with a beaming smile.

"Thank you, Amiri. I'll treasure it. Kenya will love Bollywood," he said with a giggle. With another deep breath, he turned around, tossed his rucksack over his right shoulder and proceeded towards the front door. Following closely behind, I stopped and leaned against the frame. Tito glanced back one more time with a nod. I lifted my palm in the air, sporting a warm expression, grief-stricken on the inside.

"Amir! Come on, Mahesh will be here any minute. What are you doing standing here?" Uncle Usman yapped, as he flew past me at the door like a charging bull.

It was difficult to say how long I'd been standing there in a daze. Tito had long gone.

My belongings were ready by the front door. My suitcase, my little brown blanket and a tiffin full of snacks from our neighbours. As I patiently waited for Mahesh Uncle to arrive, a sprinkle of anxiety swept through my stomach.

Beep beep! Uncle Mahesh's horn was a life buoyancy

ring, pulling me back to the shores of reality.

"Uncle Mahesh," I shouted, waving my arms in the air.

"Are you ready, Amir? Let's go," he yelled from his car window.

He hopped out and loaded up my belongings. Uncle Usman stepped outside and greeted him with a quick hug followed by a firm handshake.

"Don't worry at all, I'll drop him to the hostel doors," said Uncle Mahesh, nodding to him as he got back into his seat.

"Great! See you in the morning Mahesh. Don't forget, we are taking Diljit, his wife Balpreet and their baby girl Armeet along to the hostel too."

Mahesh Uncle nodded in acknowledgement and started the engine.

Saying goodbye to Uncle Usman was tough. Being in such an emotional state already didn't help. Unsure of whether I would even see him again, I gave him a giant marshmallow hug and thanked him for everything he'd done for me.

"Amir, I'll be seeing you in the morning. You're behaving like we will never meet again. Come on. Hurry, so Mahesh can come back quickly," he said. He lit his smoking pipe and puffed away, whilst I reluctantly perched on the edge of the passenger seat.

As the car travelled further and further down the street, I glanced back through the rear window, waving to Uncle Usman, envisioning the moment my family left weeks ago in the same manner. Another bout of anxiety and paranoia struck me. This time it was like a metal boot in my gut. *What if they didn't actually make it out of*

Uganda? What if they're in a different country and not the UK as planned? To refrain from chaotic thoughts, I began tuning into Uncle Mahesh's radio. 'Superstars' by The Carpenters was playing. Even though I was distraught and engulfed by my inner thoughts, I continued the facade of normality and calm.

"So, what do you think of this song?" Uncle Mahesh asked.

"Am I going to see Uncle Usman again?" I blurted.

There was an awkward silence. It lingered so long that it made me feel uncomfortable. Regretting my outburst, I felt the need to answer my own question out of urgency. "I'm sure I will," I nervously spurted.

"Yes, yes. He will be fine," Uncle Mahesh hesitantly responded. I couldn't tell whether he was trying to reassure me, or himself.

Another muted spell followed before 'Stairway to heaven' by Led Zeppelin began playing.

We finally arrived in Kampala. The hostel gates were heavily obscured by foliage, pockets of rust just peeping through the gaps. Lifting my head, until it bounced on the roof of the car, I caught a glimpse of what seemed like a remarkably large building block with balconies. Although it was shabby and deteriorated, there were remnants suggesting it was once a high-class hotel. We waited for a moment before a guard approached us. My nerves set in as he drew closer to the car. *Was he one of Amin's soldiers?* I thought.

"Jambo! How are you?" he asked in a friendly tone.

"We are fine, Mukasa. I'll be coming back again tomorrow with some more guests. For now, Amir will stay the night," Uncle Mahesh responded, calm and collected.

Upon closer inspection, I could see that this guard's attire was different to those of Amin's soldiers. He wore a dark blue uniform with a black felt cap, tightly fixed to his crown. A shiny baton hung off his belt to one side, along with a compact pistol, securely encased in a black leather pouch.

The guard gave me a warm, beaming smile, exposing bountiful gaps in his teeth. I couldn't help but wonder how he'd lost so many.

"Mahesh, not a problem. I'm here for the next five days on duty. Don't worry, my friend," the guard responded.

He finally opened the gates, revealing an extending driveway leading to the light grey building. We slowly inched towards the reception doors.

Asian children played happily in the gardens on either side, the atmosphere almost mimicking that of a schoolyard. They were swinging in old tyres hung from trees and playing in hammocks made from partly perished fishing nets. Seeing these young children filled with glee and contentment was comforting. Many of them couldn't understand what was happening. Perhaps they thought they were on holiday. They played so merrily and carefree in the gardens of what was to be their temporary accommodation; before they were to flee the very land they called home. In reality their lack of awareness was a blessing for them.

Uncle Mahesh hopped out and gathered my belongings from the back seat. For several minutes, I'd thought about how these children would adapt to life in another country. Whether they'd be accepted in western societies or able to adapt in a different climate. I wondered how they would overcome language barriers along with other social barriers. These were children from Hindu, Sikh and Muslim backgrounds, who'd been living together in harmony, celebrating one another's cultures and traditions. They had community cohesion running through their veins. They had the spirit of what it took to adapt. But then again, no one was really sure of what lay ahead. The uncertainty was still heavily plaguing my mind.

Uncle Mahesh and I said our goodbyes.
"I promise you, son, I'll be back in the morning with your Uncle. This is not farewell just yet," he smiled, patting my shoulder.
Hesitantly nodding, I smiled back.
As his car drove out of the gates, I expected to feel a sense of loneliness. On the contrary, I felt at ease. With the hustle and bustle of families around me, it almost felt like I was back home in Kakira.
"Are you hungry, Amiri?" the guard asked, rubbing his round protruding belly. Buttons on his uniform looked like they were about to go orbiting into outer space.
"You know, I'm starving, Sir," I said, mirroring the belly rubbing action with a side smile.
"Call me Mukasa," he said. "Follow me. The Indian ladies are making something mouth-watering in the kitchens for everyone in the hostel. I have no idea what it is, or even how to pronounce it, but it smells delicious," he smirked, leading the way.

It was almost like everyone had forgotten their woes and gained some form of escapism. By evening most of the families were gathered outside on the grass. They were relaxing on blankets laid out on the ground, enjoying a picnic kindly cooked up by many of the wives and mothers.

As the sun began to set, I once again experienced a familiar sense of contentment. Warm hues reminded me of my family and how we would gather, talking, laughing, singing.

"Let's play Antaakshri!" I suddenly spurted, taken back by my own outburst.

Everyone stopped what they were doing and stared at me for what seemed like an eternity.

"Come on then," a voice came from behind me.

"Yes, let's play," came another excited voice.

People got up, arranging their blankets on two sides of the grass, forming two opposing teams.

A little girl ran towards her father.

"Papa, what's Antaakshri? I want to play too," she chirped.

"Well, my dear, Antaakshri is a game where two teams compete to sing songs beginning with an allocated letter of the alphabet. If no one in your team can think of a song within thirty seconds, you get one strike. Three strikes, and your team loses," he said, sitting down on a blanket.

"Easy, Papa! I can help," she said, scurrying to join in.

Everyone gathered round, forming two teams. One lady brought a rusty oil can that had been discarded in the yard behind. Taking it from her, I placed it on the ground between the two teams. Grabbing two short wooden branches from nearby trees, I began drumming on the empty can. The acoustics were impressive, considering its size. The gathering resembled that of a typical Kakira wedding. People cheering, singing, dancing and children clapping their hands. Mukasa even had a little boogie before strolling back to his guarding post.

It felt like happiness, normality and safety.

CHAPTER TWENTY-SEVEN
1961 - Kakira, Uganda
Age 8

Eagerly waiting for my father to arrive home from work, I'd set up camp outside the front door with my playing cards facing the soil. The sun was my clock. Whenever it was orange, like a pot of molten lava, it was either time for school, or time to head home for the evening meal.

Ice cream day had finally arrived. Every Friday evening Adha would treat Kabir and I to the flavourful delights of ice cream from the general store in town. It was the highlight of our week. However, we were denied that privilege if we misbehaved.

Adha's car finally pulled up outside the house. I abandoned the cards and ran towards him.

"Adha are we having our ice cream today? Please, can I have mango and pistachio scoops?" I blurted with excitement.

"You can have any flavour you want, Amir. Where is Kabir? Is he ready?"

"I'm ready!" Kabir said, charging out of the house with his shoelaces undone.

Thud!

"Oh, Kabir! Your laces. The ice cream won't run away. Now look what's happened," Adha said, hoisting Kabir up, dusting down his palms and knees.

"I'm ok, Adha. Ice cream, ice cream," Kabir said.

There was no doubt, he would have been in tears had we not been setting off for delicious desserts. But he impressively controlled the quiver in his lips and held back the bucket of tears, waiting to break free.

"Ok, come on boys, let's go," Adha smiled, hurrying us along into his shiny Morris Minor. He would always give his car a clean and polish every Friday. It would gleam, ready for us to hop in and head out.

We didn't have to travel very far to get to the general store. Kabir and I would run ahead of Adha, shoving open the door of the store to see how loud we could ring the bell above.

"Hello. My two favourite customers. What flavours are we having today?" came a voice from behind the counter.

"Uncle Musa, I want the Mango and Pistachio today," I shouted, rushing to get my order in before my brother.

"Please," Adha expressed in a lengthy, firm tone.

"Please, can I have the Mango and Pistachio scoops?" I said, looking behind me for Adha's approving nod.

"Kabir, what flavour would you like today?" grinned Uncle Musa.

"I want the Tiger and Lion flavour please," said Kabir, with a cheeky smile.

"Why do you have to be such a baby? Just choose your flavour," I snapped, eager to speed up the process.

"I'll choose you a surprise flavour for now. I'm sure it will taste even better than old lions and tigers," he softly reckoned with Kabir, giving him a little wink.

Whilst Uncle Musa would fill our little ice cream cones, I would often browse around his store, inevitably drawn in by the toy section. The small collection comprised a wooden rocking horse, wooden building blocks, some handmade dolls, teddies and of course my favourite; little toy cars. Mesmerised by the radiant colours painted on them, I would lean against the shelving and gawk, hoping that someday, one would be mine.

"Adha. I really like these cars. Can I have one? Not today, but maybe one day?" I gently requested.

I was pleased with my new approach for requesting toys.

"Let's take our ice creams home. We can think about the car another time," he said.

"Me too! Kabir too," my brother called out, seizing the opportunity.

Rolling my eyes, I hurried him out of the door, once again attempting to ring the bell as loud as possible.

With our ice creams in hand, we hopped in the car and made our way home, thoroughly content with our weekly treat. They would last all of five minutes before we had devoured every crumb of the cones.

Unfortunately, the feeling of contentment was just as short lived that day. By early evening I was burning up with fever. My body was scorching, like a slim ceramic vase fresh out of the kiln. Sound became distorted; my long gangly legs had turned to jelly, and before I knew it, darkness fell before my eyes.

"Amir," a distant, distressed voice echoed.

Indistinct mumbling and cries reverberated. But I couldn't make sense of my surroundings.

In between sleep and consciousness, I'd finally worked out that I had become dreadfully ill. Turning to my mother at one point, I attempted to speak.

"Maa. What's happened to me. Where have you brought me?" I mumbled, struggling heavily with speech.

"Amir, you are in hospital. The doctor says you will be better soon though," Maa whimpered. Tears held on to her lashes, refusing to let go, like ripened fruit bearing its weight on feeble branches.

A sudden knock at the door interrupted us, prompting Maa to blot her eyes against her scarf.

"Come in, Doctor. He's conscious at the moment. Any news? Will he be ok? Is there anything else we can try? Please don't give up just yet," Maa pleaded, bombarding the doctor.

My heart sank deep into the pit of my stomach, adding to the frequent bouts of nausea.

"Mrs Majothi, with Typhoid his chances are slim. There's only one more thing I can suggest at this stage," he muttered under his breath, aware of the fact that I was listening intently.

"We need to cease all solid food intake. At this stage in his illness, he may or may not recover. We can't guarantee that a liquid diet will cure him. But it's the only option left. If you're happy to go ahead, I'll arrange for the formulas to be prepared," he gently explained.

"Yes!" Maa cried out, suddenly aware of her outburst, looking back at me with a forced, but reassuring smile. "Tell me what more I can do to help," she said.

Confusion and anxiety had left me feeling overwhelmed. Unable to stay conscious any longer, darkness fell before me once again.

Twenty-one days later, I opened my eyes. My surroundings sharply reminded me of my illness and where

I was. There was a light blue curtain draped around my hospital cubicle. After staring at the shadows of staff darting about the ward, I was alarmed by the curtain being swooshed across, revealing a stocky and stern looking nurse peering at me over the top of her petite reading glasses.

"Hmm, awake are we? Wasn't expecting that. I'll get the doctor," she croaked, as she hobbled away, clutching her clipboard.

A few moments later, Maa bolted into my cubicle.

"Amir! All praise be to Allah. Thank heavens you're ok, my baby," she exclaimed.

A few days later, I'd gathered the energy to sit up. Maa sat beside me, adamant that she feed me with her own hands.

Adha entered the cubicle with a parcel resting in his hands. Maa sat back on a wooden stool, making room for Adha to come closer. Perching on the side of the bed, he placed the little brown parcel next to my resting fingers, being careful not to catch the drip on the back of my hand.

Looking up at him with curiosity, I couldn't help but feel a warm sensation that swept through my body. For the first time, in a long time, I felt delightfully special. In that brief moment, I relished the attention I was receiving from both parents. The moment abruptly ended when my little brother came charging through the cubicle curtains.

Before I could scold him for jumping on the bed and almost tearing out the drip, he waved a small card in the air.

"I made you a card" he yelled, before catching sight of

the little brown parcel. He tossed the card aside like a magpie who'd spotted a larger piece of silver.

Adha hastily grasped the parcel.

"No, Kabir, this one is for your brother. We will get you another one. Remember what we talked about?" Adha said, wide-eyed.

Kabir glanced down, "Ok, Adha. Kabir will be a good boy today," he mumbled.

"Adha what have you brought me?" I queried, whilst examining the package.

"Have a look for yourself," Adha said, finally handing me the parcel.

It didn't take me long to tear it open, revealing an ornate, hand-painted wooden toy car.

"A car! You bought me a car. Oh, thank you, Adha."

It was an elegant blue Rolls Royce with fully functioning doors. It had the faintest aroma of wood varnish mixed with a hint of sandalwood. My fingers gently traced the texture of the handcrafted piece. I couldn't help but gaze upon its glistening surface, so delicately sanded and painted. My love for cars gave my father a sense of pride. Together we shared passion and appreciation for motors.

Overcoming an illness like Typhoid came at a cost. As a result, my left rib cage had warped inwards at an unusual angle, causing the other side to protrude outwards. I spent my childhood years masking what felt like a severe abnormality, using a baggy shirt and humour as my shield.

CHAPTER TWENTY-EIGHT

5th November 1972 - Kampala, Uganda
Age 19

As Uncle Mahesh's car pulled up to the hostel, the weight faded from my shoulders. They'd arrived earlier than expected, and I was truly relieved. Seeing Uncle Usman step out of the car that morning was a sight for sore eyes. Until I spotted his actual sore left eye, wounded arm, and the fact that he was still in his pyjamas.

"What happened?" I said, pacing over towards him.

Holding out his palm flat towards me, he immediately resisted any fuss.

"Amir, I promise, I'm fine."

"But you have a black eye. Your arm—"

"There was an incident. Early hours of this morning," he said. He glanced briefly at Uncle Mahesh, who was helping a young couple and their child out of his car. That fleeting exchange of eye contact between them filled me with dread.

"What? What is it? Tell me," I demanded.

Uncle Mahesh gave him a nod.

Uncle Usman let out a huge sigh, before finally opening his tightly pursed lips.

"Miko is dead," he said. His words hit me with one sharp blow.

It took me a few moments to register these heavy words he had just emitted. The weight of them fell so hard upon my body, my legs gave in and my knees hit the ground. I couldn't feel my hands; my gaze heavily fixed on the soil beneath me. Eventually I blinked, tightly squeezing my eyelids together, releasing the anguish that needed to escape, drop by drop. My uncle lifted me back up with his good arm and tilted up my chin.

"He saved me from Amin's soldiers. I owe him my life. It's so tragic that he lost his own in doing so," he said softly.

Uncle Mahesh stepped in, seeing that Uncle Usman could utter no more.

"Amir. They stormed into Miko's house while your Uncle and Miko were sleeping. Miko fought them off so Usman had a chance to escape. He heard Miko shout out against Amin, right to the end. Then he heard one gunshot followed by silence," he sighed.

"I couldn't stop, Amir. I took my satchel and ran. Two of them were right behind me, so I continued to run until I threw them off track," stressed Uncle Usman. I could hear the guilt in his voice. "I wish I could have done something. Miko was our friend. These devils took his life," he cried, before breaking down into the palms of his hands, leaning into my frame.

His words dawned on me and I realised that the soldiers were now in control of everything Miko had, along with all that had once belonged to us. In that one moment, I realised that the time I'd spent worrying about our property and our belongings was pointless. The anger and regret grew within me. They took away an innocent life. Our dear friend.

Why did I stay longer than I needed to? Was there any point trying to save our house? Why did Miko have to lose his life for protecting someone else's? What would happen to my sweet Rocky now that the soldiers had taken over?

"There's nothing you could have done, Usman," Uncle Mahesh gently explained, comforting him.

"Miko is gone. Our Rocky is gone. Our homes are gone." He continued sobbing.

Uncle Mahesh and I led him inside the hostel along with the young gentleman, his wife, and their little girl. Uncle Usman rested in my sleeping quarters. It gave me some much-needed time to come to terms with it all. Feelings of despair had engulfed me until a knock at the door came to the rescue.

It was the young gentleman.

"Hi. Amir, isn't it?" he whispered, aware of my Uncle sleeping in the corner.

"Yes. Diljit, right?"

"Yeah. I just wanted to bring these things over for your uncle. He helped me and my family to travel safely out of Kakira. I'm just so sad that he went through all that turmoil before he reached us. Please pass on these clothes and essentials to him from me. If it weren't for Mahesh and him, we wouldn't have made it to Kampala."

He was a very tall young man with broad shoulders. His neatly wrapped, light brown turban matched his brown tweed blazer. He didn't seem much older than me but came across as wise and judicious.

"Thank you, my brother. But why don't you give it to him yourself when he's awake?"

"We've found a lift that can get us to the airport from here, and we are leaving right away. I don't want to wake him."

We exchanged hugs and a handshake. My eyes locked on to the unusual, sumptuous gold ring wrapped around his finger; the face of a lion with two red rubies set in the eye sockets.

"That's one hell of a ring," I chuckled, before realising I could have sounded rude.

"Oh yeah. This thing. It was given to me by my father. It belonged to my grandfather. My grandparents travelled from India to Africa to work on the railways. They faced many hardships. One agonising problem they encountered was with a pair of man-eating lions. The two lions had grown accustomed to human flesh and would work together in dragging victims away from campsites, where many of the railway workers slept," Diljit explained.

"Yes! The Tsavo man-eating lions. I've heard about them. Is it a true story? I figured it was just a silly old tale the elders enjoyed scaring us with. Or scarring us with. We didn't get much sleep after that bedtime story," I smirked.

"Yup. It's true. I can confidently say that, because my grandfather was on night patrol in the camp when the second lion was finally killed and captured, before it claimed another victim," he proudly stated.

"Wow. That's impressive—and brave," I muttered, still shocked about the authenticity of a story I'd always assumed was a fictitious tale.

"He settled in Uganda, built his life here. He had this ring specially made to remind him of the struggles he faced as a young man moving from India, and the hardships of camp life. But also as a reminder that he had a fighting spirit, with the strength of a lion, to remain resilient against whatever life would throw at him. He worked hard and built a little empire selling tailored jackets. We carried on the family business."

The smart blazer he wore made more sense.

"Until now. Now it's all gone. Everything he and my father ever worked for," he sighed.

There was a sudden stillness surrounding us. Diljit glanced down at his ring.

"We won't look back. We will keep looking forward. That's what my grandfather would have said," he softly muttered, choking on his last few words.

"Diljit. No one can take our spirit. Not even Amin," I gently asserted.

Diljit gave me a nod in agreement.

"Take care of yourself, dear brother. I hope we meet again," he smiled.

"Yes, brother. I hope so too. Be vigilant. I've heard there are plenty of check posts on the way to the airport. Stay safe and look after your family."

We shook hands again before I closed the door. Looking at the time, I figured we should also do the same. We needed to get a taxi to the airport as soon as possible. No more delays. No more risks.

It was mid-afternoon before we began to prepare for our journey.

"Amir, is the money we planted in your shoes and clothing still there? Remember to keep small amounts in your pockets as a decoy," Uncle Usman reminded me.

We shared the remaining cash I was carrying. All I had to do was make sure we stayed strong and safe as a unit.

"At the checkpoints. All we have to do is be prepared," I muttered, clinging to hope and prayer for safe deliverance to Entebbe Airport.

Mukasa kindly called us a taxi. Many families were departing from the hostel with their whole lives packed in little suitcases, unsure of whether they would retain much of what they carried before boarding their flights. We exchanged pleasantries with many people I'd met the night before. The vibes were bittersweet and truly surreal.

"Good luck my friends. Don't ever forget Uganda. It will always be your home, despite what that halfwit fool Amin says," Mukasa blurted, as we climbed into our taxi.

"Thank you, Mukasa. I wish you all the best too," I said, smiling back at him.

This isn't our home anymore, I thought. *It's no longer familiar.*

Waving goodbye as the vehicle took off, we entered the next leg of our journey; our hearts filled with grief and minds riddled with uncertainty.

Our driver wasn't very talkative and seemed to be in a hurry. He briefly mentioned that he needed to head back to the hostel to accommodate many more departures before nightfall. Not that we were in the mood for any extensive conversation.

The driver soon alerted us to our first check post. Both Usman Uncle and I threw ourselves together in the middle of the back seat to get a better view, causing our heads to collide.

"Ouch! Sorry, Amir."

"That's ok. What can you see?" I mumbled, still rubbing my head.

"I can see at least three cars ahead of us. There are one, two and—three soldiers," he said.

As our taxi inched closer to the check post, beads of sweat were forming on my uncle's forehead. I continued to reassure him that everything would be fine. My gut instinct would have been to panic, but so much had happened. Something within me had changed, and I knew I had to remain calm. For my uncle's sake.

It was our turn. One of the three soldiers signalled our driver to move forward. He was immensely tall and built like a tank. He was holding his rifle in the resting position, with the barrel facing up. Without warning, he aimed it at the driver's neck. Pressing the barrel tightly against him, he demanded to see everyone's papers.

"My name is Kobe. I'm a Ugandan citizen. I'm just making an honest living transporting travellers to the airport. I have my ID card if you allow me to give it to you," the driver said, his hands quivering in the air.

"Yes, show me your card," the soldier replied. He looked back at the other two soldiers sitting on the wooden bench on duty with him, giving them a mischievous glance. They grinned back at him. One of the two seemed to have a bottle of whiskey tightly clasped, with his rifle in the other.

"Here you are, sir. My ID card."

Kobe handed his ID over to the soldier. He sneered at it before sliding it into his top pocket. Panic washed over Kobe's face, but he said nothing. He tried his best to stay calm and cooperative. *Had his card just been confiscated?* I thought.

"So. You are being used by Muhindis to drive them to Entebbe? Huh?" the soldier spat heatedly.

The situation was starting to unravel. Rather than sit back and let it escalate, I took charge.

"He's charging us triple the shillings he normally takes to go to Entebbe, Sir. After all, this is his country. Your country. You can charge whatever you like," I blurted, with a patronising undertone.

"Yes, Muhindi. We will take back our economy too. You leeches have taken too much," he snarled.

"And finally, I get to keep my hair long with no issues. The Beatles are huge in England. There will be so many long-haired fans walking the streets. My mother won't stop me then," I puffed, whilst folding my arms, staging a little melodramatic anger.

"What on earth are you saying, Amir," Uncle Usman whispered with his teeth tightly gritted.

"Go with it," I whispered back.

"Muhindi boy, you crack me up! All this calamity and all you care about is your hair? Ha ha!" the soldier snorted, unable to contain his cackle. "Did you hear that guys? This boy just wants a good hair day," he shouted.

"You know what else I want? I want to smoke," I said, pulling out a box of cigarettes from my jacket.

"You smoke!" my uncle yelled.

"Yeah. All the time. Get over it," I snapped.

The soldier was in hysterics, watching the drama unfold between me and my uncle.

"I steal your tobacco all the time too. You're just too dumb to realise it," I gibed, pointing my nose in the air exhaling my first puff.

"Ha ha. Look at your face, man. You look like you're going to explode," the soldier giggled at my uncle's expression, clearly enjoying the entertainment.

Uncle Usman sat glaring at me. I could see he was hoping this was going somewhere.

"Would you like a cigarette, Sir. My Uncle's tongue seems to have been hijacked. Plus, he only smokes pipes. Those are for prehistoric fossils," I snorted, tipping the box of cigarettes towards him.

The soldier, still finding my sarcasm entertaining, helped himself to a cigarette and returned Kobe's ID card to him. He signalled for the other soldiers to move the barriers so we could drive on.

The soldier leaned into the window, staring my Uncle deep in the eyes.

"Go! And if the boy wants to smoke in broad daylight, let the son of a gun smoke. You got that," he yelled, chuckling to himself.

"Yes, Sir," my Uncle agreed, nodding excessively.

We inched forward, slowly gaining momentum until we were back on the road again.

Each of us breathed a sigh of relief.

"So, are you really paying me triple shillings?" Kobe questioned with a Cheshire cat grin.

"Kobe, you got your ID card back. That's enough, along with the agreed fees," I smiled, feeling rather pleased with my performance.

Kobe dispensed a mischievous smirk and gave me a mini salute in his rear-view mirror.

"How on earth did he let us go without checking our papers? He just let us go," my Uncle queried, scratching his head.

"These soldiers love drama when they're drunk. They find rebellion and cheek entertaining. All I had to do was put on a little show. They're easily distracted in that state of mind," I explained, feeling rather proud of my shrewd tactics.

"That still doesn't explain why you had a box of cigarettes in your pocket. You've never taken tobacco from me. Even when I've offered it to you," he said, looking perplexed.

"Uncle Mahesh gave me these to use as a buffer. Soldiers can't resist a good smoke," I said, giving him a little wink.

"Well, you managed to divert his attention," Kobe

beamed.

We continued our journey feeling much more optimistic. We were getting closer to Entebbe until we arrived at another check post. Gradually, once again, we veered forward until a soldier leaned into the window. He was stern looking. Not that most soldiers weren't. However, this guy had a brow line strong enough to knock down a building complex. His shoulders were so broad, you could hang planets from them. He was also very sober.

"Your papers!" he demanded. His voice echoed deeper than that of a tiger's roar. Anyone could have mistaken him as Idi Amin himself, or his brother.

Kobe reached for his ID card.

"Not you, you fool. The Muhindis," he ordered.

My uncle and I immediately surrendered our passports for examination.

He snarled at the documents.

"Step out now," he ordered, repositioning his gun directly at us.

For a moment we sat there stunned at his outburst. At this point I was convinced that he was a close relative of Amin.

"Now," he growled, sounding enraged at our lack of urgency, poking the barrel of his rifle closer towards us.

We lifted our hands in the air and climbed out of the vehicle promptly. He rummaged through our pockets, taking all the spare cash he could find. We knew this would be inevitable. At least we were prepared.

"Where are you hiding the extra cash? I know you have more. You Muhindis think we are stupid?" the soldier barked.

"That's all we have. We have no more than this," Uncle Usman stressed.

"Shut up, old man! Do not lie to me, scum," the soldier bellowed.

My uncle and I looked at each other, confused as to how to respond.

"Take off your shoes, old man," he snapped again.

"My shoes? Why?" mumbled my uncle.

He fired a single gunshot into the air, making us jolt down onto our knees.

"Get up, the pair of you. Old man, I said remove your shoes now," the soldier whispered in a calm but terrifying tone.

My uncle didn't waste any more time. Hastily he removed his shoes and handed them to the soldier.

He looked inside the soles and tossed them back on the ground.

"Now show me yours, boy."

"What? Why? Look, my uncle just told you, we don't have any more than this," I stressed, trying to sound as convincing as possible. My heartbeat echoed in my ears. He wasn't falling for anything.

The soldier smashed the butt of his gun into my shoulder, causing my upper body to buckle and hit the ground. He forcefully removed my shoes. The silence that followed was chilling. I wished I could disappear. Turning to look back, I tried to read the soldier's expression. His pupils were wide and full, burning like a solar eclipse. His rage was uncharted.

"Then what is this? You lying fool!" he thundered, pulling out notes from the inside of my shoes.

The soldier gripped me by my collar and lifted me into the air. Gasping for oxygen, I tried to release myself from his mighty grip, but it was no use. I was as pathetic as a fly trying to free itself from a spider's web.

He abruptly launched my comparatively meagre frame into a leafy ditch at the side of the road. My protruding rib cage hit the ground first. Strangely enough, the landing felt a lot softer than I'd anticipated. Lifting my head, I brushed away a lock of hair that was covering my face. Looking back, I caught sight of one of the soldiers restraining my uncle, whilst another soldier began opening our luggage. Kobe stood, pleading for them to let us go.

Suddenly the soldiers weren't the biggest problem anymore. I became very much aware that the lock of hair I'd moved from across my face wasn't my own. It was much longer with the rest of it disappearing under the pile of leaves. My breathing became erratic and feelings of dread took over. Scanning the area, I noticed some brown cotton fabric, torn and somewhat bloodstained. The sight of the bloody rag prompted me to jolt up, inching myself away from it on my hands and knees. My palms at either side of me scoured for solid ground so I could stand up. But my fingers brushed against something cold buried under the leaves. Reluctantly I glanced down, identifying a bloody, bruised, ice cold hand extending out from beneath the foliage. One of the fingers was missing, as if it had been freshly amputated. When the penny finally dropped that I'd landed on a dead body, the walls of my chest closed in.

Another car promptly approached the check post. The driver exited the car and immediately sprinted over to open the back doors. A very well-dressed gentleman stepped out of the vehicle. His shoes were so shiny, I could see light bounce off them. He had a line of medals pegged on his dazzling white suit, which glistened in the blistering sun. The soldiers immediately resumed their positions and saluted the gentleman.

Unable to hear them conversing, I dusted off my clothes and stood up. Afraid to look down at the ground again, I slowly made my way towards the car, anchored in fear. Trying to stay as calm as possible, I inched my way closer to where my uncle was standing, taking slow, deep, calming breaths. He was no longer being physically detained by the soldiers. Noticing our belongings scattered from outside our suitcases, I gathered our things and placed them back in our cases. All the while, the gentleman looked to be relaying important information to the soldiers, who gave us an occasional glance. I wondered about the terror on their faces; *who could the man be, and why were the soldiers so afraid of him? Could he have been some general, like Idi Amin once was. Perhaps he was a close friend of Amin's,* I thought.

When the gentleman had finished conversing with the soldiers, they handed him a small canvas pouch. He looked pleased when he peered into the pouch, smiling back at the soldiers. He briefly pulled out some cash from the bag along with a gold chain, swiftly shoving it all back in the pouch. He rummaged to the bottom of it, as if something had caught his attention. When I set eyes on the item he pulled out, it sent a jolt of terror through my body. I keeled over and vomited.

"Amir. Are you ok?" my uncle exclaimed.

By then everyone was focusing on me.

"I—I'm fine. I just get travel sick on long journeys. I'm ok," I muttered, refraining from yelling out *'murder'*.

"I hope all is well here," the gentleman said. "I wish

you a safe journey on to Entebbe," he eerily murmured, sliding the canvas pouch into the inside pocket of his lavish suit jacket.

"Thank you, Sir," I hastily mumbled before dragging my uncle and Kobe back into the car, while we still had the opportunity.

We were relieved to be on the road again, but still reliving the trauma from the events that had just taken place like a sticking turntable.

"Are you both ok?" Kobe asked. "You took quite a tumble there, young man."

"I'm fine. My chest hurts from the fall, but I'll be ok," I said quietly, trying desperately not to mention what I'd discovered and trying harder not to vomit again.

"I thought we were goners, Amir. Who was that man who arrived on scene?" My uncle queried.

"He looked like a very important person. There have been many new officials appointed recently. Could it have been one of Amin's associates?" Kobe interjected.

"The soldiers were very quick to salute him," I said.

"Well I heard a rumour that Amin killed many of Milton Obote's cabinet members and officials, and had their bodies dumped in the Nile for the crocodiles to feast upon. Maybe these are new officials, taking advantage of the expulsion. Did you see the money and gold he took from the soldiers? Disgusting," Kobe ranted.

I however wanted to shout, *'Did you see the gold lion head ring they stole from Diljit? Did you see his dead corpse lying in the ditch? Did you see his severed hand?'*

Instead, I nodded and buried my head into my palms.

"We could have died—but Allah saved us. That wasn't our time to go," Uncle Usman sighed, still looking deeply disturbed.

The sight of Entebbe airport could not have been sweeter. My eyes welled up, and I breathed a sigh of relief. The nausea subsided, but my heart was still pounding, once again testing its true boundaries. I knew I wouldn't be at peace until we were on a flight out of Uganda.

As the taxi drew closer to the airport, we discovered that lengthy queues had gathered. The crowds weren't as large as the ones outside the embassy in Kampala. But there were many people waiting to leave with mounds of luggage.

Kobe dropped us to the doors.

"I wish you both a safe journey. Please do not worry about payment. I know the soldier took all your money," Kobe whispered kindly.

"No. They didn't," I whispered back.

With that, I tugged on the loose string dangling from the seam of my blazer's left sleeve and pulled it open. I took out the cash I had previously planted there and paid Kobe for his troubles.

Kobe burst into laughter. "Wow, that's clever. Well done. The shoe thing is common. But sewing it into your jacket—good job," he chuckled.

My uncle's grin was from cheek to cheek. He was basking in the glory of his successful planning.

"Yes, Uncle Usman. You're a genius," I groaned, rolling my eyes with a hint of amusement.

We said goodbye to Kobe and joined the queues outside, which stretched well beyond the main doors. We were in for a significant wait, but safe from check posts.

CHAPTER TWENTY-NINE
1968 - Kakira, Uganda
Age 15

It was early afternoon, and the market was in full swing. Kimo and I weaved our way through the crowds. We'd stepped on a few toes here and there, but we always slipped away through openings. I never admitted to Kimo how much I loved the market. My eyes would be pulled from stall to stall, taking in the luminous colours of sweet aromatic fruits, gleaming in the light of the sun. There was a certain enchantment about the way people moved around, like shoals of fish. The chaotic rhythm somehow seemed to flow.

"Why didn't you just say no? I hate the market," Kimo moaned, kicking a piece of rotten fruit into the gutter. "It stinks here too. The rotten food gets tossed aside in the sun to rot even more," he continued to protest.

"Maa needs eggs and tomatoes. If I don't get them, I won't get the extra pocket money I need for Dev Anand's new movie," I grumbled, waving my mother's wicker basket as if in despair. At age fifteen, it was important to hide my feelings of joy in the market, at least when my best friend was in tow. I had a reputation to protect.

"Fine. Let's get the stuff and get out of here, Miah," Kimo agreed.

Maa demanded her goods must come from her favourite stall.

"Does it really make a difference which stall we get it from, Miah. Here, look. Just buy these," he pleaded, pointing at some rather lifeless tomatoes and cracked eggs.

"Are you serious Kimo? I'm not giving up on my movie for the sake of walking a little further," I said, rolling my eyes.

Dragging Kimo deeper into the market, we headed towards Maa's favourite vendor, a young Ugandan girl called Mirembe. She handled the stall with her father. However, her father spent much of his time chatting with neighbouring vendors, smoking, and eating ugali, rather than selling fruits and veg.

"Wait. Isn't that Senyange?" I said, pointing towards a pile of dilapidated wooden crates; not far from Mirembe's stall.

"Yes, it is, and that's a bottle in his hand," Kimo replied.

"Broad daylight and he's at it again," I sighed.

Senyange heckled at a group of girls who walked past him with their shopping.

"Remember the last time we had a chat with him? He just doesn't listen to anyone," Kimo spat, obviously irritated by what he'd just witnessed.

"Let's speak to him again," I suggested.

"What's the point? He doesn't listen. He becomes aggressive if you say anything to him. Leave him be, Miah."

Grabbing Kimo by his arm, I wandered over to Senyange, who hid his bottle behind a crate as we approached him.

"Jambo, Senyange, how are you today?" I politely asked.

"Ah, Amiri. I am good. Today is a good day," he replied, attempting to straighten his posture.

"And why is it a good day, Senyange?" Kimo asked in monotone.

"You two boys will be my cupids. It was meant to be. You see Mirembe over there, selling her delicious fruit and veg?" he whispered, clearly lusting after her.

"Senyange, leave Mirembe alone. You don't want to see her when she's angry, trust me. You need to stop."

"Amiri, listen though. I want you to tell her that I love her and want to marry her," he exclaimed.

Kimo slapped his palm across his forehead. "Miah, let's get out of here," he pleaded.

"No. Wait. Let's deliver this lovely message to Mirembe," I uttered with a mischievous wink.

"Miah?" Kimo's frown transformed into a grin.

"No problem, Senyange. Leave it to me. I know exactly what to say to her. Poetry flows when you watch enough Bollywood movies," I smiled, reassuring him.

"Oh, thank you boys. Yes, use beautiful poetry to win her over for me."

"Come on, Kimo. Let's go work our magic," I chuckled.

We waltzed over to Mirembe's stall. She was busy separating the rotten fruit and veg in a wooden crate by her side.

"Hello boys. Amiri, where is your mother today?" she asked kindly.

"Hi Mirembe. She's busy with my aunt making samosas for someone's wedding. She sent me to get some eggs and tomatoes from you." I smiled.

"Of course. Let me pack it up for you."

Mirembe began wrapping fresh juicy tomatoes and some large eggs in old newspapers. She was very good at origami. She would fold the papers into little pouches, ready to fill with stock.

Our pouches were prepared, and I carefully placed them into Maa's basket after handing Mirembe her shillings.

"So, Mirembe. You know Senyange, right?" I cheekily enquired.

"Who? That drunken mess over there? Yes. I'm sick of his silly proposals. He proposes to strangers walking past him. I'm sure I saw him proposing to a car on the side of the road the other day," she snarled.

"Well, he told me to give you a message," I replied.

"Amiri, don't listen to him. He talks nonsense," she sighed.

"But he said he doesn't want to marry you anymore," I claimed, trying desperately to keep a straight face.

"And why has he suddenly changed his mind after all these months?" Mirembe chirped, putting her hands firmly on her hips.

"Well—I don't know if I should tell you the reason."

"Amiri, spit it out," she yelled.

"Well, he told me to say, *macho yako ni kama macho ya ng'ombe, na una masikio kama punda*," I relayed, before gritting my teeth together.

Mirembe inhaled deeply, exhaling harder.

"He said WHAT? How dare he?" she yelled, spilling with rage.

"Yup. That's what he said. I heard him loud and clear. He said that you have the eyes of a cow and the ears of a donkey," Kimo, chimed in, effortlessly stirring the wooden spoon.

Glancing down, I noticed Mirembe had almost filled one of her crates with rotten fruits and vegetables.

"Mirembe. You know, people like Senyange need to be taught a lesson. It's all about your actions and not your words," I suggested. Her eyes followed mine back to the reject crate.

"You know what, Amiri? You're right," she fumed.

With that, she picked up the crate and calmly walked over to where Seyange was barely standing. She rather flirtatiously giggled at him while placing the crate on the floor. Taking a handful of rotten produce, she looked him in the eyes and said, "It's not me, but it's actually YOU, with the eyes of a cow and the ears of a donkey. You fool! How dare you?" she scoffed, attacking him, one rotten piece at a time.

"Time to fly to Kimo. Let's get out of here," I chuckled.

We sprinted through the market. Once again, Kimo and I were being—well, Kimo and I. We finally took refuge under a cluster of mango trees. Unable to control our fits, we sat in a puddle of laughter.

"Miah. That was cruel what we did," Kimo laughed.

"Maybe it was. But every girl who now walks through that market will thank us," I giggled.

We looked up at the sky, perfectly framed with luscious mangoes hanging down like a decorative border.

"Ah, Miah. I think they're calling our name. Look at the colours. Shall we?" Kimo cajoled.

"May our mango adventures never end, my friend. Let's go," I cheered.

The day ended as it always did when mangoes were involved. A torn shirt, Maa's flying slipper and the subtraction of an evening meal.

CHAPTER THIRTY
===

5th November 1972 - Entebbe Airport, Uganda
Age 19

We waited several hours in a queue laced with unpredictability, trauma and loss. The crowd was in despair and tightly packed together like sardines. This was also my earliest memory of experiencing claustrophobia. Those who once had full freedom to roam vast landscapes, to feel the open-air breeze through sugarcane fields and experience the sweet taste of monsoons, became restrained; forbidden to steer away from the scant soil beneath them.

We had reached the indoor queues, finally shielded from the harsh and unforgiving mid-afternoon sun.

"You don't look so good, Amir. Your face has turned pink," my uncle pointed out.

Before I could respond, I fell to my knees.

"I need water," I gasped.

"Has anyone got any water," Uncle Usman shouted. His voice echoed in the airport atrium.

A lady wearing a pale blue saree in front of us immediately offered a bottle.

"Are you ok, young man?" she enquired, looking deeply concerned.

"I—I'm ok. Thank you so much," I replied, handing the half empty bottle back.

"Keep it. You might need it again. I have plenty more,"

she responded kindly.

My uncle pulled me up once I was ready to face the next leg of the waiting game. Another hour had passed before we reached customs. Soldiers were rummaging through people's belongings. If cash bribes weren't on the ready, then valuables from their luggage would be confiscated. We were informed on so many occasions to be vigilant of airport corruption issues and to remain well prepared. Thankfully, we still had cash sewn into various inner sections of my blazer and within the heels of my shoes.

We were up next. Two soldiers began rooting through my small suitcase. After not finding much in terms of valuable items, they resorted to hand gestures demanding money. We hastily gave them what they wanted. After sliding notes into their pockets, one of the soldiers caught sight of something. He dug his hand back into my belongings and removed my little wooden elephant.

"This is my last remaining memory of my grandfather. Please, Sir, let me keep it," I begged, clasping my palms together.

"You want it? Then pay more for it," he snarled, clasping it tightly.

Offering more cash, I pleaded with the soldier to hand it back.

"Ok, here. Take it," he hissed, tossing the elephant on the tiled floor before smashing it with the butt of his rifle.

"No!" I shrieked, dropping to my knees.

It was too late. The blow was far too forceful, causing the head to snap off.

"You beheaded him! Ha ha!" the soldiers cackled.

Carefully lifting the pieces, I delicately wrapped it in

one of my shirts, before placing it back in my suitcase.

Part of me wanted to scream at the top of my lungs. Enough was enough.

My knuckles turned white from tightly clenched fists, my teeth gritted in an effort to stay calm, and my face turned red with suppressed rage. The kind lady who'd offered me water turned around once again, observing me for a moment.

"Don't worry, child. Just a little longer. Don't react," she whispered.

She was right. It would only take one wrong move for me to lose my freedom, or my life. Keeping the end goal in sight, I let it go.

The queue moved closer to overcrowded check-in desks. It was difficult to see what was happening and noise levels were rising, causing anxious mutterings. The crowd had become desperate, flickering their passports in the air. An airline representative climbed on top of his desk, waving his arms frantically.

"Calm down. We cannot go any faster than this. Please remain calm and patient," he yelled.

The abrupt explosion of a single gunshot echoed through the building, prompting everyone to dive onto the ground.

"Stay calm, you fools, or we will take you away," a soldier exclaimed.

Everywhere I looked, I saw desperation and fear in the faces that surrounded me. No one dared to breathe. Even a falling feather wouldn't have swayed left or right for the stillness in the air. Firmly on the ground, everyone glanced at one another for confirmation of whether it was safe to stand up.

Within the passing of a few more minutes, people began to rise with caution, resuming their stance in the queue.

I could see the airline worker looked incredibly weary by this point. He tossed off his hat and ran his fingers through his hair. Looking up, he took a deep breath and extended his palm. Deciphering that as a signal for my passport, I promptly handed him my documents.

He scanned the image on my passport, before giving me a quick glance to verify it was me. He then took a stamp and pounded it against one of the open pages.

"Please move forward. You're the last one to board this flight to Stansted, UK," he murmured in a monotone fashion.

"Last one? But my uncle is with me. We are travelling together. Here, can you please take his passport for stamping too?" I stammered.

"I don't care if you have your entire family tree with you, young man! He will be on the next flight," he snapped.

"And when will that be?" I yelled.

"I don't know, boy! I don't know which airline is arriving next, or where it's headed. I'm not an encyclopedia."

Our heated conversation had piqued the attention of soldiers. In a calmer voice, I pleaded once more for the attendant to let my uncle on board, but it was no use. We had to accept the fact that we were going to split up.

"Uncle Usman, don't worry. You'll be right behind me on the next flight."

"I know, Amir. You just look after yourself and make sure you search for everyone as soon as you reach England. I'll do my best to find you wherever you are. Be brave."

We shared a short-lived hug before a soldier dragged me away by my collar and jostled me along towards the boarding gate.

"You are delaying the flight. Hurry," he grunted.

Making my way up the passenger aircraft stairs, I realised this would be the last time I set foot on Ugandan soil. Taking one last look around me, gripping the handrail firmly, I took a deep breath, absorbing the very last moments of seeing those green landscapes, those trees, and those memories. Stunned by the sheer size of the aircraft, it mesmerised me, as it was the first time I'd set foot on a plane. Having seen many movies featuring aircraft over the years, it thrilled me to be standing so near to the roaring turbines. Upon boarding, the amount of pumpkin orange that was used in the cabin furnishings dazzled me. Orange seats, orange cabin walls and orange life vests. All the seats had been occupied.

"Can I help you to your seat, Sir?" came a gentle voice. A pleasant English lady, smartly dressed in a navy-blue tunic with a matching hat, stood to my right, holding a tray filled with glasses of orange juice.

"Orange," I muttered.

"I'm sorry?" she asked, looking a little puzzled.

"Yes—I mean. Would you kindly show me to my seat, please?" I said.

She gave me a welcoming smile before guiding me to the middle of the aircraft. A cloud of uncertainty and uneasiness hung over those seated. Most window seat passengers were staring outside, their gazes locked on their last views of home.

"Here you are, Sir. This is your seat. Please call me if you need anything else."

"Thank you, Madam." I nodded. I'd never been referred to as 'Sir' before. It felt heart-warming and reminded me that humanity and kindness still existed. Taking my seat, I slid my case under the seat in front of me and firmly fastened my belt. Relieved at being allocated an aisle seat, I extended my lanky legs and stretched for a moment.

"We can rest now. It's all over," murmured the gentleman seated to my left.

"I really hope so," I answered, glancing at him.

He was wearing a cast on his right arm, supported by a strap around his neck. He was dressed in a stylish pale blue suit, with his blazer dangled around his shoulders like a cloak. Well groomed, with thick black square frames, perched on the bridge of his nose.

"Hi. I'm Dev." He smiled, extending his hand.

"Dev Anand! Nice," I grinned, giving him a quick handshake.

"Well, I'm not as stylish as him. But I try. There's only space for one Dev in Bollywood," he chuckled.

"Are you with your family?" I enquired, curious to know more about him.

"Yes. My wife is seated with my seven-year-old son behind us. My parents left Uganda yesterday. We're hoping to find them as soon as we land. But I'm not really sure what to expect. What about you?"

"My family left weeks ago. Me and my uncle were supposed to be on this flight together. I was the last one on and they wouldn't let him board. I hope they put him on a flight soon."

"Try not to feel panicked or stressed. We are all in the same boat—or plane," he said.

Glancing at his cast once again, I questioned Dev

about his arm and whether the soldiers had attacked him.

"I'll tell you once we take off. It's a great story." He grinned.

Within minutes, we were in the air. A round of applause gradually built up within the cabin. There was an immediate sense of relief with a bittersweet undertone. Everyone recognised that they were finally safe. No more brutality. Amin's regime could not harm us, and we were liberated as human beings once again. The price was our homes and all that we were familiar with. The cheering became louder, with some passengers standing up to clap.

Dev unexpectedly jumped out of his seat and removed his cast. Reaching into it, he hauled out a pile of gold and cash, waving it in the air. Passengers cheered even louder, applauding him, before his wife tugged on his clothing for him to sit back down.

I couldn't help but grin as his spouse gave him a brief lecture on why he shouldn't have done that.

"It's fine, Savitri, you stress too much. We are out of Uganda. No one will take our possessions from us now," Dev chirped.

Shaking her head at her husband's boastful act, Savitri focused her efforts on her son.

"So. You did good. I take it you have no injuries then?" I chuckled.

"Nope. Fit and healthy. But also very lucky. If they had any suspicions of my fake cast at the airport, I would have been crocodile dinner by now."

"You're lucky, Dev. Very lucky," I said with a smile.

Twenty minutes had passed. A faint murmur began to

fill the cabin. I looked around and noticed people peering and pointing out of the windows.

"We are descending," a voice shouted.

"That's right, look!" came another voice.

The plane jolted, making an impromptu turn, before it descended further. Panic swept across the passengers, prompting many to scream out to the flight attendants.

"Why are we back in Uganda?" echoed one terrified voice.

"What? Back in Uganda? No! He will kill us," another voice cried in anguish.

Leaning forward, just past Dev's shoulder, I could clearly see greenery. Thoughts of terror and doom caused me to hyperventilate. Dev saw that I was losing control, struggling to breathe. He grabbed a brown paper bag from the seat pocket and had me breathe into it.

The cabin tannoy bleeped, before an attendant made a jittery announcement.

"Could all passengers please calm down and resume your seats? We are refuelling in Kenya as President Idi Amin has denied fuel to all passenger flights collecting Asians. There is no need to panic. I repeat, there is no need to panic," she said.

"See, Amir. Just calm yourself and keep breathing into the bag."

"Okay," I mumbled, my voice barely escaping the bag.

After refuelling, we were back in the air in no time. There were no cheers or applause this time. Everyone was fed up, tired and still recovering from the short blow of distress.

"Feeling better, young man?" Dev enquired.

As my eyes scanned the cabin, I caught glimpses of

sorrow, tears, and confusion. Many were only just coming to terms with having left for good. There was no going back. Consequently, it was time to face the next challenge. Thoughts of these new hurdles plagued my mind.

Dev was still waiting for me to answer him.

"Sorry, Dev. Yes, I'm ok. I just don't know if everyone else is," I pointed out.

"Amin can take away our homes, the land beneath our feet, and our most precious possessions. But he cannot take our resilience and entrepreneurial spirit. As humans, we endure, but we always bounce back. God looks after everyone. We are hardworking people who live in harmony with all, regardless of race, ethnicity, beliefs, and other differences. Humanity is within our hearts young man, and that's all that matters. Don't worry too much about the masses. It's a scary time for all of us. But it won't be long before everyone remembers who they are and how strong they really are. It's just a matter of time."

Dev gave me a heart-warming smile and a pat on the back that sent me plunging forward.

"Oops! Sorry, Amir. You're so fragile. You need fattening up with some parathas and samosas, boy," Dev chortled.

"I'd do anything right now for my mother's amazing cooking," I chuckled, trying to mask any evidence of my despair.

We'd been in the air for over eight hours. We were treated with so much respect and dignity throughout the flight. The caring nature of the English flight attendants was comforting and well received. What started as faint whispers in the cabin, grew into nervous flurries of excitement. Once again, passengers had their gaze fixed on the windows, looking for answers to their longing questions about their new destination.

"Look, mummy they have green fields here too," cheered a little boy, waving his teddy in the air.

We had finally arrived in England. London was a place I'd always dreamed of visiting. Little did I know that I was to be sent away there. The pilot made an announcement welcoming all passengers to Britain before the plane geared for landing.

As we landed, I felt nauseous from the fresh waves of anxiety, not to mention the rocky descent. Catching glimpses from the little window, I spotted two members of staff battling torrential rain and high-speed winds in order to force the aircraft stairs in place, ready for disembarking.

Gathering my belongings, I slowly inched forward in the queues to exit. Upon reaching the plane doors, I was blasted by what felt like an arctic cyclone, scooping me up, sending my hair into a frenzy.

"It's not too cold today, you're lucky," cheered one of the flight attendants as she waved goodbye with a blindingly bright smile. She was deadly serious too.

Glancing ahead, I scampered behind the crowd, down the stairs and across the airfield. I noticed a handful of news anchors and camera operators interviewing many passengers. My goal, however, was to reach the terminal doors as quickly as possible. The cold was incredibly intense. An icy mist had seeped through my clothing, slowing down my pace. My face had become a frozen lake; solid, with little movement under the surface. Staff members were kindly welcoming all the new arrivals as we entered the terminal, ushering us towards a large hall. It was full of stations offering donations of warm clothing. Thick winter jackets and coats were being distributed. Children were also being provided with coats, shoes, socks and teddy bears.

Across the hall, a lady dressed in a special uniform gifted a beautiful handcrafted doll to a young toddler. A warm glow filled my soul, thawing me from top to toe. The smile on the child's face was enough to recharge anyone's spirit.

"And what about you, Sir? What colour would you like? We have a lot of choice," a lady called out.

She was smartly dressed, projecting a delightful smile.

"I like your uniform, Madam. It suits you," I said, before realising I was perhaps too forward.

"Why thank you, Sir", she beamed. "I'm from the Salvation Army, Sir. We've come together to help with the arrival of our new residents. Can I suggest a nice coat for you to keep warm this winter?" she added kindly.

I'd never heard of the Salvation Army. But I experienced their comfort, their warmth, and their generosity.

"What about this one?" she enquired, pulling out a long coat.

The black-and-white chequered pattern was too bold for my liking. She registered my hesitation and immediately suggested a plain brown coat with gold buttons and leather patches on the sleeves. The patches caught my eye. Most of my blazers were similar.

"A perfect fit too," I replied, slipping on the coat with gratitude.

The anguish of being in a foreign place without my family was intense, but the immense kindness I received upon arrival was soothing. It was difficult for me to remain casual with my interactions. As a result, I greeted every kind soul who handed me a donation with a bear hug. I was never a hugger. But these friendly people were the closest thing I had to compassion, safety, and love.

The masses flowed through the hall, gradually making their way to the other end, seeping out like fish from a net through the exit. We were outside again. This time, prepared for the cold.

Uniformed men were ushering families on to coaches. They gave those with young children and the elderly priority to board first.

"Where are these coaches going?" I hesitantly enquired.

"They're heading to the barracks, kid. A safe place where you can rest and stay," he said, without his gaze leaving his clipboard. "Dave! This one's full. You can get yourself off," he yelled, before clouting the side of the coach with his palm.

Motionless, I watched the coach pull away and make its way out of the airport.

"Don't just stand there, you need to get on the next coach, kid. It's too cold to be standing out here. Look, the heavens have opened," the gentleman appealed, waving his clipboard at the sky.

Heavens? I thought. *What did that mean?* Nervously, I followed his instructions, boarding the next coach in line. Finding a window seat, I took a deep breath, sank into the seat, and placed my case on my lap. Without warning, rain began to heavily thrash against the glass pane.

That's what he meant!

It suddenly occurred to me that I'd not said goodbye to Dev. Where had he gone? Could he possibly end up on my coach? Would I see him again? My eyes fixed on every passenger boarding the coach, I hoped and prayed he would climb on board, just for one more journey. Alas, the coach was full.

"John! You're full up, you can go," shouted a muffled voice from the outside, followed by a double thud. We were leaving the airport.

A young man came and sat next to me. His eyes were warm and hopeful with a hint of a smile. His hair caught my attention. It was long.

"Hi," I said, extending my hand.

"Hey, I'm Ritesh." He smiled.

"I'm Amir. Nice to meet someone with the same hair length as me," I grinned.

"Yes. It certainly is, my friend."

We were caught off guard by a lady sitting in front of us. She turned around and glared directly into Ritesh's eyes.

"You'll need to cut your hair now, Ritesh. This is England, not Uganda. You need to smarten up," she grunted.

"Exactly, Maa, this is England. You'll soon find out that everyone has long hair here. It's all about the Beatles," he chortled.

She mimicked him, clearly annoyed. "Don't you be encouraging him either," she snarled at me, before turning back around in a huff.

Trying my best to conceal all signs of amusement, I covered my mouth with the collar of my new coat.

"Don't worry about my mother. She's hated my lovely locks for a long time now. She'd take a pair of scissors and cut it herself if she could," he whispered with a snigger.

"I know that feeling all too well, Ritesh."

"Are you with your family?" he enquired.

"No, they left weeks ago. I was with my uncle in Entebbe. But we got split up. I'm hoping he turns up soon. Hopefully I'll see my family shortly. If they're still at the barracks. It's been such a long journey," I smiled with a sigh of relief.

"Oh ok, that's good. So which barracks are they at?" he queried.

Worry spread across my face, faster than syrup on a hot pancake.

Ritesh, reading my confused expression, promptly interjected. "I'm sure they are at the one we are headed for, Amir. Not long now."

"Which one are we going to? And how many are there? I thought it was just one big place," I said, watching the finish line slip further away.

Ritesh's mother turned around again. This time her eyes were more tender and compassionate. "There are plenty of barracks scattered around the UK. Some are in England, some in Wales and some as far north as Scotland. This coach is taking us to a place called Hobbs barracks in Surrey. It's located south of London," she explained.

Somehow, those last few feet left in reaching my family had transformed into hundreds of miles. The thought that they could be anywhere in the UK plagued my mind for the rest of the journey. *How many more days, weeks or months would go by without my family by my side? Did they even make it to England? Could they still possibly be in Uganda?*

The coach entered what seemed like an overgrown field leading up to withered iron gates. Two more coaches closely followed as we advanced on to the premises. Long wooden huts lined the land with white crisscross fences outlining each hut. Naked wilted trees draped over some of the huts, resting their tired branches on the roofs for the cold winter ahead. Although it wasn't raining anymore, a thick fog occupied much of the surrounding fields, with a dark hue suspended above. Stepping off the bus, I could see many people had already settled in. The place was bustling with families running out to greet the new arrivals. Most of them were searching for missing loved ones. Every few seconds I heard the wail of a mother, reuniting with her son, a father, rejoining his wife and children, a wife, finding her husband, falling to her knees, broken but relieved.

My eyes darted around the coaches, widening with hope and expectation. Scanning the hordes that had gathered, I examined them carefully, combing each individual for any form of familiarity. As the minutes passed, I was still hopeful of catching a glimpse of my mother, my father or siblings. The sharpness of a royal blue jacket stood out in the distance.

"Kabir!" I cried out, picking up speed as I forced my way through the clusters of people. My legs slowed down as I reached him. The young man turned and looked at me blankly.

"I'm sorry. I—I thought you were my brother."

I retreated before the young man had an opportunity to respond. I turned and headed back towards the coaches in disappointment. My eyes were tired from searching. I felt defeated and disheartened. The reality of displacement was paralysing me, like icy liquid metal moving through my body.

"Can all new arrivals please report to reception with your paperwork and passports? Please make your way there now," called out a deep voice from under a makeshift shelter by the coaches. A round gentleman dressed in an earthy green raincoat, tight and clearly unlikely to fasten, was pointing towards a building to the left of him. In his other hand he held a sandwich, with a colourful filling that was gradually emptying on to the ground whenever he waved his arms.

Following the horde, I moved towards the reception area. Inside, it was calm and serene. The sound of stamps on the counters echoed in the wooden hut. There was a strange damp smell that filled the air with a hint of an unfamiliar chemical.

"Next!" a clerk piped from behind her desk.

Shuffling over to her, I placed my case on the ground and handed her my passport. She kindly acknowledged me before recording my details in a large, distressed leather notebook. Her tiny frames sat on the tip of her nose, almost about to plunge off the edge, before she inched them back with her pinky finger, continuing to note my information.

"Right, young man. We have assigned you to hut number twelve, room B. This is your camp ID card, so never leave the grounds without it. A member of staff will visit you in your room later this evening to give you more information about the barracks and help you with anything you need. Hot drinks and snacks are available in the food hall until dinner is served this evening," she stated, handing back my documents and a new ID card.

"Thank you, Madam. Would you know if my family is staying here? They should have arrived in England weeks ago. I'm hoping to find them," I implored.

"Sir, I understand. But the best way to check is by visiting the family board further down the hall. Names of all the families staying in these barracks are listed there. Other barracks do have some listings present, but they are not all up to date yet, as you can imagine."

A glimmer of hope remained. Making my way to the boards, my soul filled with anticipation. But sadly, none of the names I searched for were recorded anywhere. Deflated once again, I made my way to my allocated room in hut twelve. The room contained four single beds, each one with a neatly folded blanket placed on a single crisp white pillow. Three of them had already been occupied, with luggage stacked around them. Placing my case underneath the empty bed, I rested myself on the edge and planted my head deep into my palms.

"Amir, it could be worse. You're lucky to be here and safe."

I looked up to find Ritesh leaning in through the door.

"They're not here. I checked on the boards for their names," I murmured, flopping my hands upon my knees.

"Look, you will find them. Just try to get some rest for now. Lucky for you, I'm staying in this room. I'll keep you entertained," he said with a smile.

I wanted to respond, but there were no words to convey my exhaustion and heartache.

"Hey, guess what? My portable radio works here. I picked up some amazing stations. Wanna listen?"

He tuned his radio, discovering a very clear transmission of 'Get back' by none other than The Beatles.

The irony of the lyrics had us glaring at each other until we burst out into laughter.

"If we *'go back to where we once belonged'*, we'd be in

serious trouble, Amir," Ritesh chuckled.

CHAPTER THIRTY-ONE

1964 - Kakira, Uganda
Age 11

"Miah, you're too slow," Harman bragged. He was already on the first set of branches, picking juicy jambus.

"I'm right behind you, don't you worry," I smirked.

It was hard to see where my footing was that night, but we'd had our eyes on this particular tree for days. We just needed to find an opportune moment to climb it without getting caught by the proprietor of the luxury home.

"These guys look filthy rich," Harman whispered.

"Hope no one's awake—or we'll be dead meat," I chuckled.

Harman had filled his pockets and began digging into the jambus.

"Can't you wait till we get home to eat? You're so greedy."

"Miah, you still need to pick yours. Hurry up so we can—"

Harman froze.

"Harman, what is it? Are you ok?"

His eyes fixed on the roots below us, his index finger pointing to a moving entity.

"That's a snake," I shrieked.

"Not just any snake, Miah. That's a Black Mamba," he whimpered.

It proceeded further up the tree, its armoured body glistening in the moonlight as it slithered closer. A single Mamba's venom could kill not one, but a large group of people. Its bite was considered to be the most fatal of all snake bites in Africa. Without rapid significant treatment, it was impossible to survive.

Harman began to shake. The jambus he had firmly grasped in his hands fell to the ground. This must have aggravated the snake, because it raised its head and hissed intently. Its dark tongue flickered in the light; its focus firmly fixed on its prey.

"Harman, we have to move back. We have to show the snake we aren't confronting him."

"Miah, the only way is down, and right now, that's not an option."

"I know. We have to back up on the branches. If we fall, we fall. But it's the only way out of this."

"What! Have you lost your mind? We'll break our bones!" he gasped.

"Yes, but at least we'll live."

"Okay look, you go left and I'll go right. One branch won't take our weight together," he groaned. We headed off in opposite directions. Glancing back, I could see the Mamba effortlessly gliding closer, with its victims clearly in sight.

We carefully backed ourselves up to the very ends of our branches, until we could feel the tension weakening.

"Miah, mine's not going to hold. I'm going to fall," he screeched.

"Just keep quiet and stay as still as you can," I slurred, my insides tightening with each second.

Alas, the snake had made its way to the top. It looked left and then looked right, its tongue still flitting in the air, tasting our sweat and fear.

Without further ado, it slithered its way towards Harman.

"Miah. Miah!" he whined.

Numbness had engulfed me.

"I'll have to jump, Miah."

Preparing for his urgent plummet, he scanned the ground for a potential landing site.

"Those leaves. I'll aim for the leaves, Miah. I'm going to break my legs today. All for these stupid jambus," he cried.

"Harman, look!" I whined, sharply gesturing towards the snake.

It had made a U-turn, now inching closer towards my branch.

"Miah. Jump, jump!" Harman shouted, his voice shaking.

The snake had locked eyes with me. It had become a game between predator and prey. If I didn't jump, I'd lose my life. If I took the plunge, then I could break a leg, or worse.

"Harman, we jump on three. No questions, no hesitation," I ordered.

"Oh my God. I can't do this, Miah."

"One!"

"Miah, this is so bad, I just can't—"

"Two!"

"Miah!"

"Three!"

We descended with a synchronised sharp thud, tossing surrounding leaves high into the air.

"Harman, are you ok?" I spluttered, muddy and grazed as I tried vigorously to rub away the pain in my left shoulder.

"Miah, we made it. Woo hoo!"

The snake abruptly pelted its body down to the ground, eager to catch its victims. Grabbing a handful of jambus, we each howled and sprinted out of there as fast as a cheetah behind its prey.

Once again, we were running with fruit in our pockets, our hearts clobbering against our chests and sweat dripping down our foreheads.

"That was close, Miah. That was crazy close!"

CHAPTER THIRTY-TWO

6th November 1972 - Hobbs Barracks, Surrey, UK
Age 19

Rays of warm sunshine greeted my eyes through the cream net curtains. My lungs expanded and my heart filled with hope. Braced and ready for the challenges of the day, I sat up to find Ritesh and two other young men tuning into his radio for music channels.

"Hey, sleepy head. How are you doing this morning?" he asked.

"I'm good thanks. Ready for another day, I guess," I mumbled, twiddling my fingers around the corner of my duvet.

"This is Azar and Sahil. They're in this room with us. You fell asleep pretty quick last night, and I didn't get a chance to introduce them."

They gave me a smile and continued to fiddle with the radio.

"So, where's your family staying?" I enquired.

"Ah, they're in the hut across from ours. Couldn't fit us all into one. It's better, trust me. I can play my radio as loud as I want in here, without my parents jabbering on." Ritesh laughed.

"Have I missed breakfast? What time is it?" I asked.

"Nah, you'll never miss a meal here. There's always something in the food hall. We'll come with you. Come on," Azar said, putting on his shoes.

The hall was busy, but large enough to cater to the whole camp. Folding tables with little wheels were aligned in long rows with seats at either side. Many people were perched with cups of tea and plates of toast. A queue had formed at the far end where staff members were serving breakfast. Taking a brown plastic tray, I joined the queue, whilst the boys grabbed a seat. They'd already had their fill earlier that morning.

Waiting patiently, I took my tray under my armpit and began tapping out a beat. Engrossed in a rhythmic trance, I almost missed what the gentleman serving food was asking me.

"What can I offer you drummer boy?" he said with a smile.

"Oh, I'm sorry. Yes Sir, could I have some toast and tea please?"

"You can call me Brian, kid. And of course you can. Coming right up," he smiled.

Brian was at least six feet tall and had the build of a wrestling champion. He displayed an unusual tattoo on his left arm of a bull's head.

Handing my breakfast over, he gave me a friendly glance.

"That's my star sign, Taurus. But I tell people it's my spirit animal," he said with a wink. "I play the drums in my spare time. You've definitely got rhythm there, boy. Keep it up."

"Oh, that! That's just old habits. I'm always tapping on cupboards, chairs, worktops, you name it. I used to play a lot in Africa," I said coyly.

"Well, you know, they do shows here, evening entertainment. We could do with a drummer or a guitarist."

"I play guitar too!" I burst out, realising I'd prompted others in the queue to turn around.

"Well, that's great. You can play some of that Indian stuff. I'm sure the others will love it," he suggested.

Giving him a polite bow, I proceeded to my table and told the rest of the boys what the canteen staff had proposed. They were just as excited as I was.

Later that afternoon, word had spread that another coach was due to arrive. By the time the vehicle had entered the grounds, the area was thronged with families searching frantically for their loved ones. I stayed back and observed from a distance. It was much easier to scan the crowds that way, instead of becoming immersed in a sea of distress and confusion. It wasn't long before a voice called out from behind me.

"Amir."

I turned around to find Uncle Usman standing behind me, with a small bag clutched in his hands, and the biggest smile pinned from cheek to cheek.

CHAPTER THIRTY-THREE

2nd January 1973 - Hobbs Barracks, Surrey, UK
Age 19

My uncle and I would check the notice boards every day, searching for clues to discover which barracks my family could have been in. With each passing week, hope was like a flickering flame in a cruel arctic wind. By the eighth week, it had reduced to a dying ember. I was convinced that they'd not escaped Uganda.

That morning, I sat on the edge of my mattress with my duvet still around me, feeling an unsettling numbness; like a ghost with a hollow shell for a body, running through time. Being without my family made me realise how fragile life is. In one moment, you can live in heaven surrounded by love, and in the next, life can leave you feeling so isolated and disposable.

The brutal weather outdoors was too much to endure. Much of my time was spent wrapped up in my coat on top of half a dozen extra layers to keep out frosty chills.

Climbing on to my mattress, I peeked outside from the window with my duvet still tightly clutched and my elbows resting on the decayed wooden sill. Snow was falling; I couldn't believe my eyes. It was something I'd only ever viewed in movies and magazines. Children were rushing outside to catch their first ever snowflakes upon their un-gloved little hands, with their parents in tow, frantically waving jackets and hats in the air. Each snowflake danced with such grace, as if choreographed by a subtle breeze. Winter was in full swing, with its icy serenade bringing merriment to the residents of the barracks, who'd quite frankly never dreamed of seeing its purity or enchantment in the flesh.

"Amir. Are you ok?" Ritesh called.

Looking behind me, I saw him popping his head in from behind the door.

"Yes, my friend. I'm fine. Just watching the snow falling. I'm coming to terms with the fact that my family didn't make it," I said, glancing outside again.

"You don't know that, Amir. You can't give up just yet. It's going to take some time. Think about how many of us have been displaced. It's a lot of people to organise," he said, closing the door behind him.

"My uncle and I have been checking the boards every day. The other day I thought we'd found them, but when we asked reception to phone across, we discovered a spelling error. Wrong family," I sighed.

"But at least more and more names are being registered on the notice boards every day. It's just a matter of time. Trust me."

Ritesh tried his best. I admired his spirit, and his efforts to lift mine. He was lucky to have travelled with every single one of his family members. Although he often jibed about wanting his own space away from them, it wasn't difficult to see how much he loved them.

"Amir. Let's go get some breakfast. The boys are going to meet us there."

Reluctantly, I put on my shoes and jacket, and followed Ritesh over to the canteen hall. Brian was on duty again, serving food. He acknowledged me with a wink before I sat down with the boys. They chatted away whilst playing with a deck of cards on the table. Ritesh gave me a nudge as I'd zoned out.

"Come on, Amir, it's your turn. I thought you loved card games," Ritesh giggled.

"Not anymore. Those days are gone," I said, before leaving my seat. "Just going to get some tea guys. I'll be back."

As my feet carried me over to Brian, I'd hoped I hadn't offended the boys. My heart just wasn't there.

Brian was busy mixing some eggs into a bowl. As I approached him, one slipped out of his hand and splattered on the floor.

"Whoops. My second one this morning. These sausage fingers don't help mind you. Anyway! Drummer boy! How are you today and what can I get for you?" he asked cheerfully.

An awkward silence descended.

"My mother, my father, my two brothers and my sister. That's all I want, Sir," I mumbled.

"Son—" he sighed. "I know it's hard. But you've got to have hope."

"Hope? What's hope? A little gentle fairy that's going to magically open the door to happiness?" I chirped.

"No. Not at all, boy. Hope isn't a magic fairy or whatever you just said. Hope is putting on a pair of boots and kicking that bleedin' door down yourself. Understand?"

Brian's outburst startled me. Wide eyed, I continued to stare.

"A change of attitude and a brave step forward in that

fog. THAT will bring you hope," he said, handing me my morning tea.

We exchanged smiles as I nodded in appreciation of his wise words. He was right. Surviving those past five months was a battle I never thought I'd have to fight. It was up to me, how I envisaged the next part of my journey. Hope had to remain grounded.

Later that night, an entertainment show was to take place in the hall. All the tables were wheeled away into storage and brown plastic chairs were aligned in rows, facing a clearing, or what would be the staging area. Two heavy lights were propped on tripods, highlighting centre stage. By eight o'clock, the hall was filled with colourful saris, clapping hands and tapping shoes. A young man called Balvinder had just played some wonderful Bollywood songs on the guitar whilst the crowd sang along. Nostalgia parachuted me back to the weddings of Kakira once again. The cheering, the warmth, the melodies; all of it was revived in that hall.

"Next on stage, we have Amir, our drummer boy. Give him a warm welcome, everyone!" cheered the hostess.

The hall became a sea of applause. People had been waiting patiently for me, having warmed to my weekly appearances.

Unexpectedly, I caught sight of my uncle waving his brown blazer in the air behind the back row. He was flapping like a bathing magpie, thrashing its feathers. His lips were trying to mouth some words, but I couldn't make any sense. Yet a rush of adrenaline engulfed me, forcing my stage-ready superstar posture to wilt.

After excusing myself to the hostess, I exited the

bright lights and headed to the back of the hall. A low humming swept over the audience, with children questioning their parents about why the drummer boy was suddenly leaving.

My uncle took me by the arm and smiled.

"I've spotted your father's name on the board. He's in Gaydon Camp."

My eyes widened as my mind registered his words.

"Come on—let's ask reception to call him," he urged.

With every step, my sprint transformed into an uncontrolled slide across the icy yard to the reception hut.

"Wait for me, Amir," my uncle shouted, trying not to slip on the newly formed ice rink.

"Come on. Hurry!" I chuckled, as he fell flat on his bottom.

"For heaven's sake, Amir. You go. I'm going to take my time, thank you very much," he scoffed, steadying himself up against the bark of a tree.

"I'll meet you there," I giggled.

Stumbling into the reception hut, I dashed over to the desk and asked the lady seated there for details about my father. Her little button nose was buried in a large diary with her squinting pupils less than a centimetre away from the tip of her pen. She continued to complete her sentence before acknowledging my impatience. Short and stout, she was perched on a light brown leather swivel chair that was boosted up to the highest position it could handle. Despite this, her eyes struggled to see past the top of the counter.

"Yes, young man. I'll call Gaydon Camp now for you," she sang. Her voice was soft and melodious. She proceeded to dial the number, lacking any urgency. Each swish of her index finger in the dial spool was like a mellow dance; her pinky finger stiffly pointed outwards. "Yes. I'm inquiring on behalf of a young man here at Hobbs Barracks, who is seeking his father. I believe he's registered at your facility. A mister—"

"Ismail Majothi," I hurriedly interjected.

"I—I'll spell it for you," she hesitantly murmured.

"Yes. That's great. Yes. Ok. Yes, we will wait," she said, handing the phone to me. "Here. They're calling him. Won't be a moment, dear."

Taking the phone, I took a deep breath and prayed it would be him this time.

Uncle Usman shuffled in, still rubbing his grazed buttocks.

"That's going to hurt in the morning," he said, clearly unimpressed by my haste. He raised his eyebrows upon seeing the phone in my hand.

"Is it—"

"I don't know yet. They've gone to call him," I said. Our eyes locked together in a trance of uncertainty.

"Hello? Amir?" a hesitant voice spoke.

"Adha! It's you!"

"Amir! Thank God you're ok."

My lungs filled with fresh air. My shoulders slumped before tears departed from my glistening eyes.

In the background, I heard Maa begin to weep.

"I'm fine, Adha. Uncle Usman is with me. We've been searching for your name for weeks. Is everyone okay?"

Uncle Usman came closer and put his ear against the speaker.

"Everyone is safe and well. We are all together. Mahesh Uncle is here. He told us how you took care of everything with Miko. The house, the help and Rocky. He sang your praises."

My uncle and I glanced at one another.

"We—we did what we thought was best, Adha. Miko—Miko is happy and well. He'll be looking after our home with Rocky. He sends his regards and best wishes to all of you."

Part of me was crumbling inside, all the while I remained composed. I intended to follow the story that Uncle Mahesh had told them. The truth would have broken their hearts.

"I'm proud of you, my boy. Above all, I'm so glad you're here. We made it, Amir. We made it."

EPILOGUE

Amir was reunited with his parents and siblings at Gaydon Camp in Warwickshire. After being housed in various locations around the UK, the family eventually settled in a small town in West Yorkshire. They were joined by Uncle Usman, who was also reunited with his family from Kenya.

Amir's mother and father lived happily together, as their children moved on in life to have families of their own.

Aziz moved to Norway to settle down with his wife. He had two children.

Kabir went on to achieve a great career as a driving examiner and got married to a beautiful young lady from Kenya. Together they had three children. Kabir's preference of domestic pets changed from chickens to cats.

Shafina stayed local and settled close-by to her broth-
˙, Amir and Kabir.

˙ir managed to track down many of his friends in
 including Kimo, Harman and Niraj, and also
 ˙ globe, as far as the USA. He has remained in

touch with many of them, with reminiscent get-togethers and phone calls. Thankfully no shenanigans have been re-lived.

Amir settled down with a charmingly beautiful young lady, originally from Kenya, living in Kent. He then focused his efforts on studying at London School of Electronics. He built his career as an electronics technician and computer hardware genius. He went on to have two children, one of whom often posted slices of jam toast into his VCR player as a toddler. Thankfully, his skills set came in handy.

His daughter, Noreen Nasim, was particularly keen to preserve his story in the pages of a book after having a daughter of her own. She was eager to write and share this extraordinary piece of history with her family and the world. She believed that bravery and resilience should be honoured, and that these exceptional stories of life should be celebrated for generations to come.

I love you with all my heart dad. I salute your bravery and resilience, and I'm so proud to be your daughter.

~Love Coco-doll

P.s. Sorry I screwed up so many of your VCRs. I hope this makes up for it. Xxx

ACKNOWLEDGEMENTS

A heartfelt thank you to my father for coping with my consistent flow of questions. You shared your stories in such a unique way, that the narrative became easier for me to portray. You let me share your story of courage and bravery with the world. Thank you Dad.

A warm thank you to my loving mother, Naeema and my brother, Arif, who have always supported me and expressed their confidence in me.

Thank you to my amazing husband Adil for the immense amount of love and support you've given me. You brought me the best cups of tea when I'd be perched on the edge of my chair, writing for hours on end. Your encouragement and love allowed me to achieve what I wanted.

Thank you to my aunty, Jaswant Jutley, for being my source of inspiration and a role model I've aspired to my whole life. You lived through this cruel historical event and yet your spirit is as tenacious as ever. You went from being a Ugandan expat to receiving an MBE from Her Majesty The Queen. I couldn't be more proud of you.

uge thank you to my bestie, Oliver Reeve, for keeping
ane throughout my writing process. Your encour-
nt and positivity played a great part in reminding
ep moving forward. Dude, you're the best.

A big thank you to my friend and famous author, Craig Hallam, for inspiring me to write. You've lit the flame.

Last but not least, a heartfelt thank you to my editor, Amy Wilson. You helped cultivate this book as if it were your own. Your caring nature and attention to detail made it an absolute dream to work with you. There are no words that can help me convey how much gratitude I have for all your time and effort in helping me to bring this story on to the pages of a book; one so close to my heart. Thank you, Amy.